Yes, You Can...
Find More Meaning in Your Life

Create a Positive Attitude,

Physical, Financial and Social Well-Being

and a Passion for Knowledge.

YES, YOU CAN...
FIND MORE MEANING IN YOUR LIFE

Create a Positive Attitude, Physical, Financial and Social Well-Being and a Passion for Knowledge.

BY JACK JONATHAN
AND SHEELAGH G. MANHEIM, PhD

ILLUSTRATED BY PAUL COKER, JR.

Discover the good life!™

STOWERS INNOVATIONS
— INC —

An American Century Company

For a hopeful author, going into a large bookstore can either be a source of inspiration or a challenging experience: so many books, so many ideas. We were fortunate to have enthusiastic supporters who helped us from Jack Jonathan's first concept, through the writing process, and finally, to the publication of our book.

An advisory board gently helped us shape our ideas, suggested the Pause for Reflection section, and were very supportive. It was a pleasure to review our progress with them and hear their helpful critiques. John and Sharon Blevins, Connie and Charlie Fox, Loriann Clayton-Bethard, Rev. Donald Sears, Jeannie Himes, Dr. Alan D. Forker, SuEllen Fried, Glenda Spellerberg, Vicki Franklin and Linda McMahon: thank you.

One of the goals of our book was to inspire people to find meaning in life despite challenges and setbacks. We were encouraged by Bob and Karen Brush, Mike Dearing, Vicki Franklin, Dr. Stan Friesen, Charles Gusewelle, Dr. Bill Neaves, Maggie Neff, Rosemary Smithson, Tina Sprinkle, Rose Stolowy, Jim Stowers, Peggy Wrightsman, and John Wurst who shared their experiences. It was not only a privilege to talk with each of them, but their insights added meaning to the content of our book. We thank them for their time.

We were fortunate to have had several dedicated editors, who suggested major revisions. Miriam McCartney often challenged our viewpoint which sharpened our insight and led us to clarify the message. Alexis Preston had a keen eye for the order and flow of our thoughts. Kate Wilkinson and Nancy O'Neill were of great help in polishing what we felt was our "final" draft. We are deeply grateful to the four of you, our book's "grandparents."

Once again, Paul Coker agreed to enlighten our readers with his marvelous illustrations which helped to keep us from taking ourselves too seriously.

We would like to give special thanks and recognition to Mary Grant, who gave us permission to publish, for the first time, two of her heartfelt poems, "Making it Through the Night" and "My Home by the Sea."

Finally, we are indebted to our trusty Stowers Innovations "team" of Sam Goller, Alexis Preston and Frank Addington. They were very patient with the constantly moving target of our completion date. It was a relief to turn our manuscript over to their capable hands, knowing that it would finally be published.

Jack Jonathan and Sheelagh Manheim

March 14, 2005

When you are financially secure, it is easier to

afford the care you need to stay healthy.

"Yes, You Can… Find More Meaning in Your Life" will help you reaffirm what is good in your life. Along with financial well-being, the book will focus on other essential aspects of a meaningful life: positive attitude, good physical health, social relationships and a passion for knowledge.

You will discover that each of these main elements supports the others. When you are financially secure, it is easier to afford the care you need to stay healthy. When you are healthy, you have more energy to follow your dreams and cultivate your relationships. If you have a positive attitude, you are more likely to manage your money wisely, share yourself with others and have a passion for life.

This book will provide you with words of wisdom and stories from real life experiences. It will stimulate your curiosity to take a closer look at yourself and the world around you. Illustrations by Paul Coker will tickle your funny bone with wry views of the challenges and joys of living.

When your passion for life is undiminished, you will discover that *The Best is Yet to Be.*®

James E. Stowers

James E. Stowers

Founder, American Century Investments
Co-Founder, Stowers Institute for Medical Research

I realize that my whole life has been a relay race with myself.

"The circle of life is like a running track

on which we run our one and only race."

In 1938, when I was a young man, my team won the Egyptian National Championship in the 4 x 100 meters relay race. We were on our way to the 1940 Olympics! One of the keys to our success was a technique first used by the American relay team in the '36 Olympics in Berlin. Each team member, running at top speed, was prepared to receive the baton within a prescribed space along the track. Looking back, I realize that my whole life has been a relay race with myself. As I move to each new stage in my life I prepare for it by finding my stride, so the inevitable change is as smooth and seamless as possible.

Each relay team member has special skills that are best for different stages of the race. One person is good at getting off the mark fast; one goes around corners best; one is good on the straight-away to the finish line. Likewise, in life, we are more suited to certain skills at one time than another. For example, in our early years we are physically vigorous and have a great capacity for learning; however, the older adult may have acquired wisdom that comes with experience. The key to running a smooth life race is to prepare, while at the height of one stage, those skills that will be needed to carry us smoothly on to the next stage. We don't want to drop the baton. But if we do, we want to be able to pick it up and keep on moving forward.

I believe that our purpose in life is to fulfill our potential and to help others. To enjoy a meaningful life, we need to open our hearts and minds so we can discover new ways to experience our world. It is our passion for life that helps us to be self-renewing and vibrant.

This book was written to reexamine the qualities we value in our lives which we may have taken for granted. The world around us is changing fast. It may sometimes feel like we are losing our footing and we start looking for ways to find balance and harmony.

Yes, You Can… Find More Meaning in Your Life is a thoughtful guide to finding equilibrium. Its aim is to be informative, inspiring, insightful, and ultimately, empowering. It deals with down-to-earth issues, while encouraging us to seek our hidden potential. Fortified and inspired we will become more resilient, able to overcome setbacks and achieve those things we never believed possible.

To get the most out of our lives we need to be aware of those fundamentals that support us along the way. We also need to reaffirm our strengths and examine our weaknesses at each stage of our life. We can prepare ourselves well ahead so that we can stay flexible enough to meet unexpected challenges. The circle of life is like a running track on which we run our one and only race. Make your race one you will run with fulfillment and happiness.

Jack Jonathan

It Is Never Too Late To Plant Redwood Trees

> *Deathly ill with bronchitis, facing the dire financial stress common to businessmen in the Depression, my Grandfather Hope announced to his grandson that he would plant an avenue of redwood trees and live to see them grow tall. It was 1938 and he was 74 years old. Ten years later, he had recouped most of his fortune, and the redwood trees had grown tall. He died in peace.*

I grew up with relatives who lived with full vigor until they were nearly 90. It is no surprise, then, that I have always expected to work at what I enjoy until I die.

When Jack Jonathan invited me to help him write *Yes, You Can ... Find More Meaning in Your Life*, I found it easy to say "yes" because we both have a similar world view. We have even read many of the same books and articles over the years.

I am a social scientist, and Jack is a creator and developer of new ideas, so we speak with different "voices." We have woven our ideas together with the viewpoints of those we interviewed, a cartoonist, poets, and scientists, to create the richness and harmony of a full chorus proclaiming the good news that life is abundant and meant to be lived until the end. I believe this diversity of sources is the charm of this book. We hope you will find a message in our book that speaks to you and inspires you to discover, or continue to develop, what makes life a moving, meaningful experience for you.

May you find joy in your life, and may your flame burn long and bright.

Sheelagh G. Manheim, PhD

Part One - Positive Attitude 19

Foundation of Well-Being

A positive attitude is central to happiness: the feeling that all things are possible, that YES, YOU CAN enjoy life if you are determined to. The key to authentic happiness is to develop your strengths of character. We believe that the most important element in forming a positive attitude is an understanding of yourself and human nature. Knowing yourself, and relying on your strengths, you will be able to adapt and cope with the inevitable changes life brings.

Part Two - Physical Well-Being

The first step in supporting our physical well-being is to cultivate our senses. Are we as careful in maintaining our minds and bodies as we are of caring for our cars? Most of us are not. Sometimes we are shocked at the consequences of this neglect. Yet it is never too late to adopt a lifestyle that will not only maintain our health, but may help us regain some of what we have lost through neglect.

Part Three - Financial Well-Being

"Salud, pesetas, y amor, y tiempo para gozarlos." Spanish Proverb

This old Spanish proverb helps to put financial well-being in perspective when we consider what makes a meaningful life. It advises that we need "Health, wealth, love and time to enjoy them." For most of us, accumulating financial assets is like a marathon race between time and our ability to build up enough resources to make it possible for us to do whatever we want to do when we want to do it. When we have a sense of financial well-being, we are really free to focus on finding more meaning in life.

Part Four - Social Well-Being

It is necessary to nurture our relationships throughout our lives. The support of close family ties and the comfort of long-term friendships are enriched when we cultivate relationships with people of various ages. Older individuals can be stimulated by associating with young people. Younger people can gain wisdom and compassion by interacting with an older friend or mentor. The skills we use to foster close relationships will also help us relate better to everyone in our lives.

Part Five - Passion for Knowledge

We are a work in progress. A passion for learning is the spark that keeps our mind alive even if our health fails or we are unable to keep up our social contacts. This quest for knowledge can bring passion and joy to us all our life long. It becomes an investment in ourselves and others which pays off in terms of happiness and better health. Then we can find the joy in sharing our knowledge with others so we can have the satisfaction of knowing that the relay race will continue when we pass the baton.

POSITIVE ATTITUDE

Foundation of Well-Being

It takes discipline and determination to
  choose positive over negative feelings.

"The goal of life is not just survival, but well-being."

Antonio Damasio, M.D.

Mind and Body

In the seventeenth century, the French philosopher, Rene Descartes asserted the supremacy of the mind over the body when he wrote: *"I think, therefore, I am."*

This pronouncement was the rallying cry of the Age of Reason. Yet, even in Descartes's time, there were some who did not entirely agree with him. For example, Spinoza, who was born in Holland only 36 years later, would more likely have said, "I think I feel, therefore I feel that I am." Recent research by Antonio Damasio, a distinguished neurologist, has shown that indeed the basis of logical thinking is feeling.

The mind and body are inseparable and act upon one another. Thoughts, feelings and desires are inextricably linked to the way a body functions. Yet we are generally unaware of the countless changes that are going on in our bodies. What we do know is that a positive attitude will often accelerate healing and renewal; conversely, a negative attitude can be a factor in breakdown and deterioration of mind and body. More startling is the fact that **it is within our power to transform a negative attitude into a positive one and in so doing change the course of our lives**.

Self-Awareness

To thine own self be true
And it must follow, as the night the day,
Thou canst not then be false to any man.

William Shakespeare, Hamlet

Mind/Body Dualism

The first doctrine of Western biomedicine (now considered out of date) was the doctrine of mind-body dualism, instigated by 17th century French mathematician-philosopher Rene Descartes. This is the idea that the physical body is completely separate from the mind, soul and other less tangible factors.

Adapted from:
Charles F. Longino, M.D.

Positive attitude begins with self-awareness. When we know ourselves, it then becomes possible to maintain a positive frame of mind no matter what the circumstances. Asked what she feels makes up the "good life," Rosemary Smithson, President of the Missouri Women's Caucus, said that it all begins with knowing yourself. She continued:

Well, I think it's a combination of things. Number one, you have to get to know yourself and be at peace with who you are. And then you can go from there. And whoever you are, and whatever it is, it is okay... Not everyone is going to like you.

Make your own way. And make your own little rules. You have to get to a point where you realize it's okay to do that. But it is also important to listen to criticism, evaluate it and then decide if it is right for you.

...the process of knowing ourselves begins with the sense of our physical well-being and how we respond to events and people around us.

Emotions come from a physiological reaction to something in the environment or our mind. Then our mind reacts to what is happening in our body. Only then do we have thoughts and feelings. Therefore, the process of knowing ourselves begins with the sense of our physical well-being and how we respond to events and people around us. As we become conscious of our emotions we can understand what contributes to our happiness or discontent and deliberately improve our state of mind. Finally, we can appreciate the impact our attitude and actions have on others.

When we understand our feelings and can control our moods the personal happiness and well-being that result will affect the well-being of those around us. **It takes discipline and determination to choose positive feelings over negative ones.**

Rehearsing the Right Attitude

In 1942, I was a young man in Alexandria, Egypt, coping with the daily stresses of keeping a printing supplies shop open; nightly wartime curfews; and the pressure of trying to live each day as if nothing had happened the night before.

On my way home in the darkness of the blackout, I would walk the long beach, listening to the waves, whose steady rhythm drowned out the sound of the air raid sirens and the anti-aircraft guns defending the Alexandria harbor.

I would examine the way I had behaved that day. Then, I would conjure up and rehearse the right approach to inspire confidence and patience in the clients I would serve the next day.

Upon arriving at home, 4 miles later, I would write on a 3 x 5 card the key points I wanted to keep in mind for the next day. In this way, I was able to cope and maintain a positive attitude during a very stressful time.

Jack

This approach can also be valuable if we are anxious about upcoming events. We may more quickly redevelop a positive attitude if we counteract our anxiety by planning ways to cope with potential problems. We may not always be in control of what happens, but we can control the manner in which we deal with it.

Self-Awareness Leads to a Change in Attitude

"Only as you know yourself can your brain serve you as a sharp and efficient tool."

Bernard Baruch

Sometimes we find ourselves responding inappropriately because our emotions are triggered by events. If we can be aware of our reaction, we can take control of our mood and change it before we hurt ourselves or others.

Feelings Underpin Our Lives

"Feelings are the continuous musical line of our minds, the unstoppable humming of the most universal of melodies that only dies down when we go to sleep, a humming that turns into all-out singing when we are occupied by joy, or a mournful requiem when sorrow takes over."

Antonio Damasio. M.D.

Here is an example of how I was able to control my emotions under tense circumstances.

I knew the man was mistaken in his view and grew annoyed. Although I thought I had confronted him gently, I noticed that the group was pulling away. The two of us were left alone.

I heard my voice, which, although quiet in tone, had acquired a very hard edge. The effort to keep my voice soft had created tension in my throat and I felt as if I was growling! I became aware of my threatening expression and apologized to the man. I then found a more socially acceptable way of communicating my difference of opinion.

The man did not immediately respond to my apology and I was aware that my critical tone had caused ill feeling. I followed up with a written apology. When we met again, he greeted me with a smile.

Sheelagh

> *The tone with which we communicate is critical to the impression we make on people and the way they will relate to us.*

It is difficult to hear our own tone of voice. Yet the tone with which we communicate is critical to the impression we make on people and the way they will relate to us. The words we use convey only 25% of what we mean. Voice tone and body language convey the other 75%. Paying attention to the way others respond to us is often our first clue that what we are saying is being clouded by our body language.

Are your arms crossed over your chest?
You may appear guarded.
Is your body turned away?
You may seem uninterested.
Is that person backing away from you?
You may be perceived as too aggressive.

When we become self-aware, we can correct impressions that do not match with the message we want to communicate. When we are consistent with our words and our body language, people will be more at ease with us.

Find a time and place where you will not be interrupted.

Most folks are about as happy as they make up their minds to be.

> *"To be happy is to experience life not as a series of struggles but as a gift, one that has no known limit."*
>
> John Tarrant

Happiness: A Key to Enjoying a Full Life

Some people are born with a natural tendency to be happy. You can observe this in infants. When they are only a few weeks old, they will look up at their mother and smile! Happiness is mirrored in the contentment of the baby warmed by the comfort of its parent's love. We are born to be happy.

One of the qualities of happy people is that they are able to see the "big picture." Opportunity seems abundant and life seems to smile back. On the other hand, unhappy people have a narrow perspective. In their book ***What Happy People Know***, Dan Baker, PhD and Cameron Stauth comment:

Unhappy people tend to see things in absolute terms and often cannot distinguish small problems from big ones. Happy people see shades of gray, and they know how to prioritize their problems and turn them into possibilities. They don't lose sight of life's big picture during bad times.

The research in positive psychology has shown that happy people are more likely to enjoy a fulfilling life in every way. In his book ***Authentic Happiness***, Martin Seligman, PhD, lists some of the benefits of a positive attitude:

- Happy people have better physical resources.
- Happy people have better health habits than those who are unhappy.
- Happy people are more productive and have a higher income than those less happy.
- Happy people endure pain better and take more health and safety precautions.
- Very happy people have a richer and more fulfilling social life than unhappy people.

Happiness results in more productivity.

Hostility Hurts Our Hearts

One of the physiological changes that is related to hostility is inflammation of the arteries. This inflammation shows up in tests for protein released by immune cells. Men who score high on hostility also have higher levels of tumor necrosis factor in their blood. Inflammation of the arteries around the heart is called atherosclerosis which we know causes heart disease.

Research by Edward C Suarez,PhD
James G. Lewis, PhD, and
Cynthia Kuhn, PhD

Contrast these benefits with the fact that people who are prone to anger and hostility are three times more likely to have a heart attack than those who are not as angry. In general, hostile people have a higher incidence of heart disease, high blood pressure, and premature death. They have more conflict in their close relationships and less social support. Furthermore, angry people put their spouses at risk for heart disease because of the stress of dealing with the hostility and the marital problems that result.

People can deal with anger either by expressing it or by repressing it. Whether they deal with their anger or not, people who experience anger will have a rise in blood pressure. However, it is the **holding on** to anger and hostility that increases the physical problems that lead to heart disease.

Changing Anger to Peacefulness

Many psychologists and social workers teach anger management. For example, a recent guidebook by Kassinove and Tafrate outlines a model of four steps for changing or reducing anger:

- **Prepare for change** by being aware of anger and finding a motivation to change.
- **Change angry responses** by learning to be assertive instead of aggressive, by avoiding situations which lead to anger and by learning to relax in tense situations.
- **Learn to be more accepting** of others; forgive instead of carrying a grudge.
- **Maintain the changed behavior** by monitoring new situations which may trigger anger.

For those of us who are afflicted by temporary moods of sadness or anger, altering our outlook may not be as simple as making up our minds to do so. However, we can modify our behavior, which will result in a change in our feelings. As children, when we were sad or grouchy, our mother might have told us to put on a happy face. We were told that when we are afraid we will feel more brave if we whistle.

Recently, scientists have been able to explain this powerful interaction between our behavior and our feelings.

I remember how I was able to whistle my way out of feeling sad and anxious when I was a young man in Egypt.

Whistle a Happy Tune

Many years ago, I was working late and had to study for exams. I felt stressed by my job and the anxiety of passing the exams. I suppose the stress showed because a Hindu captain who sat across from me on the bus asked why I was unhappy. I told him how difficult things were at work and at home - trying to earn a living when I had never earned a living before. He gave me some advice which I have never forgotten. He said if I went home feeling this way the whole family also would feel bad. He said I could change my state of unhappiness and anxiety by acting happy. He told me that after I left the bus, I should start whistling a tune of a beautiful song and whistle it all the way home. I followed his advice. By the time I rang the bell, I was in a totally different frame of mind.

Jack

We feel better if we whistle.

Authentic Happiness: A Growing Asset

The previous story shows how I created a feeling of authentic happiness simply by changing my behavior. Of course, the problems remained, but I was now able to view them from a different perspective.

The ability to control our mood helps us develop self-confidence and resilience in the face of difficulties. Lasting happiness is really a habit we can build by cultivating our strengths. It is the happiness based on these strengths of character that transcends us and touches people around us.

It is true that we can temporarily feel happy when experiencing a new sensation or sensual pleasure. However, people who practice gratitude, altruism, humility, humor and other positive traits develop inner resources and strengths which

The ability to control our mood helps us develop self-confidence and resilience in the face of difficulties.

inspire confidence. Practicing these strengths will help us to develop an emotional well-being that cannot be induced artificially.

As Charles Gusewelle, a columnist for the *Kansas City Star*, remarked, *"Character is the most important thing in life."* We may feel our life is good when we become aware of what pleases us and when we take time to really experience life. However, most of us want more than just a pleasant life; **we want a meaningful life**, which we achieve as we develop strengths and inner resources. Each of us has signature strengths that, when used every day, become the basis of an authentically happy life.

In his book on **Character**, the philosopher J. Kupperman, PhD, argues that to have a good life one needs a strong and good character. To have a very good life, one needs a life that is meaningful, with long-term commitments and projects.

Gratitude is a Strength

Gratitude is a way of looking at life with thankfulness and appreciation. Although some people seem to be more naturally grateful, it is an attitude that can be carefully cultivated.

Bob Meneilly, founding pastor of Village Presbyterian Church in Prairie Village, Kansas, feels that gratitude is the mother of all virtues. Dr. Meneilly lists five things that can help us live life with an attitude of gratitude:

- Keep a daily gratitude journal. List the things for which you are grateful.

- Make a conscious effort to thank people.

- Do at least three things for others every day.

- Find humor in your life every day.

- Spend time with people and things you are grateful for.

When we are aware of our blessings, we enhance our well-being and are a blessing for those around us. When her children were little, Sheelagh helped them fall asleep by having them count their blessings instead of sheep.

Every night as I tucked each child into bed, I would ask, "What do you have to be grateful for today?" Instead of dwelling on what had gone wrong, each child fell asleep with a smile, thinking of the good things that had happened that day.

All of us can benefit by being aware every day of the small and large things for which we are grateful. Focusing on life's blessings helps us to be resilient in the face of difficulties. An attitude of gratitude also inclines us to be generous to others.

Karen Brush is a person whose gratitude for her good life inspires her to reach out to help others in her community. Here she describes her desire to support her family, but she talked just as passionately about wanting to help strangers.

I am so grateful to my in-laws for the support they have given my husband, Bob, and me. Now, as they face health problems, Bob and I would like to reach out to them. My mother-in-law is reluctant to accept our help; but I feel so strongly that it is time for us to give back.

Karen's sentiments reflect the fact that gratitude and altruism are two sides of the same coin; when we feel grateful for what we have, we want to share our blessings with others. As we share our bounty, we develop a sense of connection and belonging, which increases our emotional well-being. **We are grateful for having been able to share.**

Forgiveness: A Kindness to Ourselves and Others

People who feel gratitude for life are often the same people who are able to be generous and forgiving. To forgive means to "renounce anger or resentment against someone." If we are able to do this as a way of life, Fred Luskin suggests we may live *"with an experience of peace and understanding that can be felt in the present moment...a powerful assertion that bad things will not ruin our today even though they may have spoiled our past."*

The wisdom of the world's religions and philosophies teaches us that we ourselves have the most to gain by being forgiving. Yet, for most of us, forgiveness is something we have to cultivate because it is not always easy to be forgiving. It does

5 Stages of Forgiveness

1. Experiencing a loss which leads to negative emotions which feel justifiable under the circumstances.

2. Becoming aware that feeling angry does not feel good and it is time to move on.

3. Remembering how good it felt in the past when you were forgiven.

4. Becoming aware that you have a choice about how long you remain resentful.

5. Becoming a person who forgives as a matter of course.

Fred Luskin, PhD
Senior Fellow Stanford Center
on Conflict and Negotiation

not matter whether we are hurt deliberately or unintentionally, we instinctively want to fight back. How can we forgive if we have been willfully and intentionally hurt? Are we to "turn the other cheek?"

Pain and suffering are real and it takes a generous person to be able to rise above it. Yet, as Everett Worthington, PhD, director of "A Campaign for Forgiveness Research," points out:

Resentment, one of the core elements of unforgiveness, is like carrying around a red-hot rock with the intention of someday throwing it back at the one who hurt you. It tires us and burns us. Who wouldn't want simply to let the rock fall to the ground?

Forgiveness has to happen before healing can take place. People who are able to forgive feel happier because they relieve themselves of the burden of resentment, which clouds their attitude and can make them bitter. **It takes a lot of energy to hold on to hate.** Therefore, to forgive is really a gift to ourselves because it releases negative energy and frees us up to enjoy life.

It takes a lot of energy to hold on to hate.

Forgive and Forget?

In order to forgive, we need to understand the reason for the other person's hurtful behavior. Then, perhaps, it will be easier to forgive. Yet, even when we understand and forgive, **we may never forget**. Forgiveness does not mean forgetting or denying that painful things occurred. It does not mean being reconciled to the loss. Furthermore, it does not mean we have to forgo seeking justice. Forgiveness means to lift a burden from ourselves by letting go of the past and its resentments, and becoming grateful for our present.

Patience and Tolerance

"Patience. In time, grass becomes milk."

Chinese proverb

Patience is defined as an ability to tolerate delays and setbacks. Those who are blessed with this quality seem to take life in stride and are not inclined to "sweat the small stuff." Impatience may just be a bad habit or it could be the result of an irritable disposition.

The good news is that the virtue of patience can be learned.

- Slow down and give yourself time to think.
- Listen and understand what it takes to perform a task.
- If a situation causes impatience, change the situation if possible.
- If you can't change the situation, change yourself by accepting what is.

When we develop the virtue of patience, we find that not only do our relationships with others improve but also our self-esteem and feelings of well-being.

The first thing for me when I am faced with adversity is that I'm not going to let it beat me. The next thing is, I try to take the problem and analyze it. Number one, is it really a problem, or is this something that you perceive as being a problem?

A lot of times we think something is a problem and it's actually just a matter of misconception, it's not really a problem. I also believe in patience. Just because something rears its ugly head in front of you doesn't mean that with patience and understanding you can't smooth it out.   Mike Dearing

Patience is defined as an ability to tolerate delays and setbacks.

"Take time to laugh…it is the music of the soul."

Old English saying

Mr. Dearing equates patience with being stubborn and determined, not giving up on people or a tough project just because things don't go well at first. **This is patience with teeth.** It is the wisdom to persevere, to wait with respect, attention and understanding, until the correct action becomes apparent.

Humor as a Strength

Norman Cousins's account of his attempt to overcome a deadly illness illustrates the powerful effect of the mind on the body. In his book, ***Anatomy of an Illness***, Cousins, the former editor-in chief of *The Saturday Review of Literature*, describes what happened when he was diagnosed with a terminal illness. He began to experiment with vitamin C, which was said to boost the immune system. His belief in this "miracle" vitamin was so complete that he had it injected intravenously. These large doses of vitamin C did help him, but he was not cured; there seemed to be something missing that his body needed.

He had read about the powerful effect of laughter on the mind and body. Could this be the missing element that would stimulate his brain to improve his immune system? So, in his hotel room, he watched old movies: Charlie Chaplin, Buster Keaton, Laurel and Hardy, and other great comedies from the silent era. He laughed. The combination of vitamin C and laughter created a chemical reaction in his brain which built up his immune system defeating the disease. Laughter, which he later called "inner jogging," did lead to a physical change which in turn enabled his body to overcome the disease.

Fortunately, we are not all confronted by such life threatening reasons to be light-hearted. Finding reasons to laugh at ourselves or our situations during the day just makes life more bearable.

Rosemary Smithson is founder and volunteer with the Women's Political Caucus in Missouri where she and others mentor women who want to run for political

"We do not stop laughing because we grow old, we grow old when we stop laughing."

Giacomo Spero

office. She works hard to inspire these women and can sometimes get too earnest. "Good grief, lighten up," she'll remind herself. For Rosie, life is an adventure that is energized by her terrific sense of humor and optimism.

In fact, every situation in our lives can be a source of humor or discomfort, depending on the way in which we view it. When we can see the light side of an event, it can give us a sense of release which helps us accept and deal with circumstances that may have seemed too difficult for us to handle.

An e-mail currently making the rounds indicates that the Japanese take this principle seriously! One Japanese company has replaced the normal Microsoft error messages, with humorous haiku poems (fixed lyric form in 17 syllables). Here are a few to tickle your funny bone.

> Chaos reigns within.
> Reflect. Repent and Reboot.
> Order shall return.

> Program aborting,
> Close all that you have worked on.
> You ask for too much

> Yesterday it was working.
> Today, it is not working.
> Windows is like that.

Reflect for a minute. Wouldn't getting such a message diffuse your irritability with programming errors!?

Laughter is such a valuable health resource that one physician in Bombay, India, began an experiment in which he deliberately induced laughter in people using a series of laughs based on yoga poses. Madan Kataria, MD, said, *"Laughter puts you in a positive state of mind and brings hope."* There is now an organization based on his work called Laughter Clubs International.

Take Two Jokes and Call Me in the Morning.

Laughter is good medicine. Look at this list of benefits of a good belly laugh and run right out to your local video store to stock up on great comedies.

Laughter is a good prescription for better health because:

- It increases breathing rate.
- Increases blood circulation.
- Increases heart rate.
- Decreases blood pressure.
- Decreases the level of stress hormones.
- Increases pain tolerance.

From an interview with
Mike Sager
AARP, July/August 2003

Humility

Humility is the quality of not feeling more important than others. True humility comes from the belief in the intrinsic value of everyone.

Great leaders have the ability to influence people, not only from the height of their station, but also from a sincere appreciation and respect for the value of others. They acknowledge the influence of those who came before them, and are appreciative of the inspiration and talent of those who have worked with them. People who are humble do not seek the spotlight, preferring to let their accomplishments speak for themselves.

The great scientist Isaac Newton expressed humility in this quote from his memoirs:

> *I do not know what I may appear to the world; but to myself I seem to have been only like a boy playing on the seashore, and diverting myself, in now and then finding a smoother pebble or a prettier shell than ordinary, whilst the great ocean of truth lay all undiscovered before me.*

Many successful people are aware of their accomplishments, yet remain humble. For example, a writer, well-loved and known in his community, had this to say about his columns:

> *You don't get it right every time. But you have to be forgiving. You just have to get up every day to do the best you can that day and say that's what I did.*
>
> Charles Gusewelle

Charles Gusewelle does not sit down to write with the idea that he is a "wise" and helpful person. He is simply telling the stories of his life, hopeful that what he says will be of interest to others. In so doing, his column touches others.

No Big Splash

These words were used in an obituary about the world's oldest mountain guide who died at age 103, June 14, 2004.

"Here was a man who climbed not for individual glory, but to help guide others safely up the mountains. You have the feeling that he was not trying to be the best. He was just climbing mountains because he lived in them, and he was there, not to make a big splash."

The Economist
June 26, 2004

There is No Indispensable Man
Saxon White Kessinger

Sometimes when you're feeling important,
Sometimes when your ego's in bloom,
Sometimes when you take it for granted,
You're the best qualified in the room.

Sometime when you feel that your going
Would leave an unfillable hole,
Just follow this simple instruction
And see how it humbles your soul.
Take a bucket and fill it with water;
Put your hand in it up to your wrist.
Pull it out, and the hole that's remaining
Is the measure of how you'll be missed.

You may splash all you please when you enter;
You can stir up the water galore;
But stop, and you'll find in a minute,
That it looks quite the same as before.

The moral in this quaint example
Is to do just the best that you can.
Be proud of yourself, but remember,
There is no indispensable man!

A perfect example of humility:

- Do your best.
- Be proud of your accomplishments.
- Don't let your success go to your head.

Enthusiasm Touches Everyone

Enthusiasm literally means "the God in me" from the Greek "en theos." When it is a sincere extension of our character, it is contagious and energizes those around us. Peggy Wrightsman is the embodiment of enthusiasm and vitality, inspiring the people she meets and works with. When asked what resources she had to help maintain her positive attitude, she said:

I feed myself by being surrounded by people I enjoy. I sincerely love my job. Every day I come to work it is fun. If it is not fun, I make it fun. I live with no regrets. I don't say, "I'm going to do this tomorrow," because the right timing never comes. So I take advantage of opportunities and enjoy them. I have four children who are like my personal filling station. They help balance my life.

Dale Carnegie, the author of ***How to Win Friends and Influence People***, taught the value of enthusiasm in his opening morning sessions. To create an enthusiastic frame of mind in the participants, he would have them pound a rolled up newspaper into the palm of their hand while chanting in unison "act enthusiastic and you'll be enthusiastic." This kind of enthusiasm is expedient, but short-lived. True enthusiasm needs to come from within or the sincerity and its effect are missing. **People feel the difference.**

The enthusiastic person lights up the imagination of others. Jim Stowers, founder of American Century Investments, exudes both enthusiasm and optimism. He often ends his public speeches with "The Best is Yet To Be®." When he says this, you know he means it. You can hear the enthusiasm in his voice.

Hope is Like a Lighthouse

"Hope is like a lighthouse. It must be built on a solid foundation, able to withstand storms and send a beacon of light to ships in distress."

Christopher Reeve
Actor

Hope for Life

"In the depth of winter, I found there lay within me

an invincible summer."

Albert Camus

From the dawn of civilization, man has been supported by feelings of hope. A farmer seeds his crops and hopes for rain. A hunter ventures forth with his bow and arrows and high hopes for a good hunt. It is part of human nature to hope that providence will favor us with abundance. The poignant song in the musical ***Annie*** talks of the sun coming up tomorrow. This little orphan has to have hope for a better day in order to endure the desperation of her situation.

We cling to hope when confronted by difficult moments. On these occasions, the support of a good friend can strengthen our faith that, yes, we can overcome adversity. **When we have hope, everything seems possible.**

A man was diagnosed with melanoma, a form of cancer serious enough that it is often considered terminal. Any one of us, in such circumstances, hope to be numbered among the 10 or 20% who survive. A friend, visiting him in the hospital, composed this haiku poem which not only gave the man hope at the time, but still sustains him nearly 20 years later.

It is noon on a bright, clear, late winter day. Looking from my bedroom window I see a stretch of meadow covered with a blanket of snow. A line of fresh footprints dots the landscape. As the warm sun shines on the meadow, the footprints slowly melt, revealing the wet grass which sparkles in the sun with the promise of spring, and hope for a new life.

> *May your troubles be*
> *Tracks in the snow,*
> *Melting in the springtime sun.*

When someone offers hope with sincerity and love, it can help us overcome setbacks and inspire us with renewed **hope for a better day**.

Hope for Life

People who view aging as a positive experience live an average of 7.5 years longer than those who look at it negatively…In any given year, studies indicate pessimists have a risk of death 19% greater than average. The power of optimism is even greater than that of lower blood pressure or reduced cholesterol.

Becca R. Levy, PhD
Psychologist

TIME FOR REFLECTION

Happiness

Consider your overall mood. On average what percent of the time do you feel:

Happy _____ %

Unhappy _____ %

Neutral _____ %

What triggers your feelings of:

Happiness _____

Unhappiness _____

Whistle a Happy Tune

What strategies do you use to change your mood?

An Attitude of Gratitude

Think of things (even small things) you have to be grateful for today.

Forgive and Forget?

Think of an instance from your life when your ability to forgive set you free. Were you able to forget the pain as well?

Patience and Tolerance

What helps you remain patient?

What do you do when people are intolerant of others in your presence?

Count Your Blessings

Studies have demonstrated that the simple mental and emotional focusing technique of counting one's blessings yields psychological and interpersonal benefits.

Reported in *Research News & Opportunities in Science and Theology*

Lighten Up!

Where do you find humor in everyday life?

What makes you laugh out loud when you are alone?

Humility

Describe someone you know and admire because of their humility.

Enthusiasm

What or who are the "filling stations" that help maintain your vitality and enthusiasm?

Hope for Life

Think of a time when special friends gave you hope.

What role does hope play in your life?

> **Authentic Happiness**
>
> *"We want to be entitled to our positive feelings...Positive emotions alienated from the exercise of character lead to emptiness, to inauthenticity, to depression, and, as we age, to the gnawing realization that we are fidgeting until we die."*
>
> Martin Seligman, PhD
> Psychologist

Reflecting on his life, Jonathan Winters advises us to live every moment to the best of our abilities. Live every day like it's going to be our last. But above all, he advises, "Keep your sense of humor."

From an interview with Mike Sager in *AARP*, July/August 2003

DETERMINATION

You, too, can reach your goals...

　　if you are absolutely determined to do so.

"Today's mighty oak is just yesterday's little nut

that held its ground."

Anonymous

Gentleman Jim Corbett was, in his time, the best boxer ever to step into the ring. He was a master of the art of self-defense. In his autobiography, Corbett pointed out that each fighter has the same equipment: two arms, two legs, a body and a head. What, then, is the secret that makes one man a champion? Corbett's answer:

"Fight one more round."

> *When your legs are so tired you have to shuffle back to the corner of the ring,*
> ***fight one more round.***

> *When your arms are so tired you can hardly lift your hands to come on guard,*
> ***fight one more round.***

> *When your nose is bleeding and your eyes are black and you are so tired you wish your opponent would crack you on the jaw and put you to sleep,*
> ***fight one more round.***

> *Remember, the man who always fights one more round is never whipped.*

Gentleman Jim Corbett (1866-1933)

Corbett practiced what he preached. In his first fight against John Sullivan in 1892, he won in the 28th round! Jim Corbett found the strength to persevere because he was determined to end his fights a winner.

You, too, can reach your goals...if you are absolutely determined to do so.

One Step at a Time

"Great works are performed, not by strength, but by perseverance. He that shall walk with vigor three hours a day, will pass in seven years a space equal to the circumference of the globe."

Samuel Johnson

Setting Goals

"There must be a goal at every stage of life."

Maggie Kuhn, founder of the Grey Panthers

...just dig out all the jobs that you have sidetracked and stuck in your left desk drawer and get them done.

Setting achievable goals is crucial to success. If we set our goals too high, we may get discouraged. If they are not high enough, the feeling of accomplishment is diminished. The most satisfying situation is when our goals and our determination drive us to succeed beyond our expectations.

Sometimes a big goal is unreachable. We may begin to feel discouraged or frustrated. Some of us procrastinate by fiddling around. This is the time to set a small easily attainable goal. When we break a big goal into smaller incremental goals, it gives us a way to achieve success and, therefore, motivation on our way to the ultimate goal.

The founder of Hallmark Cards, Joyce Hall, expressed this same idea when he wrote this memo to his employees in 1957:

When I was a boy, they used to give me sassafras tea this time of year to thin down my blood and "to get you to feeling good." Unfortunately, they found out that sassafras tea had nothing to do with making you feel good and as far as I know they don't use it anymore. Too bad...because it was kind of a nice thing to believe in.

But, if you want to feel good, I know a surer way...just dig out all the jobs that you have sidetracked and stuck in your left desk drawer and get them done. That will not only make you feel better than the sassafras tea does, but probably help other folks who are held up by the procrastination of the job you haven't finished.

Of course, this advice is more difficult to follow if the goal we can't reach is the dream of how we want to live our lives. In these situations, to avoid feeling defeated or depressed, we may need to modify our plan. For example, a man who had a successful law practice had to give up his cherished career to run the family business when his father was ill. He managed to improve the business beyond his father's expectations. When asked about the sacrifice of abandoning his ideal career, he simply said, *"If we cannot realize our ideal, then we can idealize our real."* By embracing the reality of changing circumstances, he managed to redirect his ambitions and "idealized his real."

Striving for Your Personal Best

> *"I do the very best I know how, the very best I can;*
> *and I mean to keep doing so until the end."*
>
> Abraham Lincoln

In the book, ***Zen in the Art of Archery***, there is a passage in which the zen master is teaching the pupil to shoot. After exhaustive practice, the pupil is able, in one fluid motion without glancing back at the target, to draw an arrow from his quiver, insert the arrow in the bow, turn and release the arrow toward the target.

It takes a great deal of determination and practice to reach our target in an effortless motion. First, each step must be learned individually. When our body masters what to do in each step, the mind lets go, and allows us to perform the many steps as one.

Likewise, when we set a goal, we do not focus on it at all times, but rather, knowing it is there, proceed step by step to achieve it.

> *"I select individuals who will have the persistence to stick with it in spite of the fact that sometimes experiments may fail."*
>
> Bill Neaves

In 1962, Mr. Hall wanted to inspire his staff to keep on trying even when others did not believe they could succeed. He was reminded of the Wright brothers, working away in their bicycle shop, hearing passers-by daily telling them, "It won't fly, Orville." Fortunately for us, the Wright brothers believed in themselves and their project, and, after much trial and error, the biplane DID fly.

To inspire his staff, Mr. Hall had a table tent designed, illustrated with the Wright brothers' first flying machine and bearing the phrase "It Won't Fly, Orville." In the morning, all the executives found it on their desks: a reminder from Mr. Hall that they could do more than they thought possible.

Determination and perseverance are the character traits which, when combined with a positive attitude, help us to reach our personal best.

Encouragement Feeds Determination

"Determination is the glue that holds

our character together."

Giacomo Spero

We are strengthened in our resolve when someone recognizes our potential. The story of the invention of the Xerox machine illustrates how having a champion helps us maintain our determination in the face of obstacles. The inventor of our ever-present office copier, Chester Carlson, worked for years to get his invention to function reliably. He tried to get big tech corporations like IBM to support him in his research and development. Finally, Carlson got the the president of Haloid, Joseph Wilson, to risk his company's future on the copy machine idea.

Finally, in the 1960s, the determination and vision of the two men became a reality. The copy machine, named the Xerox, became a roaring success. David Owens remarks in his biography of Carlson, *Copies in Seconds*, that "Invention is the mother of necessity." Wilson's long-term enthusiasm, support, and commitment to Carlson had paid off, not only for the two of them, but for the world.

The Stowers Institute for Medical Research is dedicated to producing basic research for the benefit of all of mankind. Bill Neaves, President and CEO, chooses his researchers carefully from among the world's top scientists. He also takes his role as cheerleader for this group of dedicated, brilliant researchers seriously.

> *I select those individuals who have an innate commitment to hard work and making discoveries. People who are marathoners rather than sprinters; who will have the persistence to stick with it in spite of the fact that sometimes experiments may fail. Then, I express, as opportunity permits ... optimism and encouragement that things will turn out well in the end if they just continue to pursue the good ideas that they are after.*

In fact, most of us thrive on the expectations and admiration of others to support our dreams and fire up our determination. When we were children, our parents clapped and cheered at our efforts at mastering new skills. As we grow, we continue to look to others for encouragement even when we are steadfast in our determination to reach our goals. As adults, that recognition may come in the form of a raise or an award. But, best of all, it could also come as a smile of admiration and pride from our family and friends.

When we were children, our parents clapped and cheered at our efforts at mastering new skills.

Resilience

"An ability to recover from and adjust easily
to misfortune or change."

Webster's Dictionary

We can picture ourselves as bamboo reeds that can withstand storms of wind, rain, and ice. Bamboo bends but cannot be easily broken. Like a reed, we also can overcome adversity by being flexible. When we are in a troubled emotional state or when we struggle through chronic illness or pain, we find the strength to go on and thrive. Our will to overcome and accept these setbacks is a part of our being and an expression of our resilience.

I think it is simply positive thinking that helps me be so resilient. When things are tough I know something else will emerge tomorrow, something different. I see life as a constant series of challenges. I have to find out I can do things, so I look forward to challenges. I look for them.

Peggy Wrightsman

Building Resilience to Stress

Resilience is really a process that can be taught, even though it may seem like a genetic trait. For many people today, life is too fast, too busy, too loud, too timebound. An accumulation of small stresses can combine to generate enough distress to cause emotional and physical breakdown. Resilience and self-reliance will be strengthened when we learn to prevent stress from becoming unmanageable and debilitating.

Each decade has had its favorite "remedies" for relieving stress. In the 30s and 40s the glamorous movie stars were often depicted using cigarettes and alcohol. They became role models for many of that generation, so that relieving stress by smoking and drinking became common. In the 70s and 80s it was

...relieving stress by smoking and drinking became common.

popular to cope with stress by "playing hard" on the weekend to compensate for "working hard" during the week.

Today, weekend retreats have become popular, as well as spas and cruises. Although these self-help treatments may ease stress temporarily, none can relieve the damage of long-term stress. It is important to build resilience to stressful situations by managing stress all day long.

Here are simple ways to reduce stress and prevent it from becoming unmanageable:

- Breathe slowly and deeply from your abdomen.
- Relax your muscles, especially around your neck, shoulders and belly.
- Get up and move around for a few minutes.
- Listen to music that is slow and low in tone.
- Relax your mind by imagining a beautiful scene.
- Get some new perspective on the situation that bothers you.
- Shift your focus from short to long by looking into the distance.

One of the most important sources of support in times of stress is our network of friends and family. They can strengthen our determination to persevere and help us develop resilience.

A family who had an infant born with severe problems likes to help out at the Ronald McDonald house because they know what that kind of quiet support means in times of stress.

We were in the position once where we were really worried about the health of our child who was ill when she was born. When you have a child in intensive care it just means so much to have a hot, home-cooked meal. So, our whole family is involved in cooking for the Ronald McDonald house. This suits us because we can do it ourselves with no fanfare. We make meals, take them to the hospital, and set them up for the families so that they have a home-cooked meal. Glenda

Laughter in Poverty: Resilience

"There is a toughness in our kind, an adaptability and tenaciousness that keep us scrabbling up toward sunshine against all odds," observed Leonard Pitts Jr., reflecting on his visit to the abject poverty of a Freetown slum in Niger. He was commenting on the resilience he witnessed in the laughter of people and the playing of the children who were living in this *"poorest nation of the poorest continent on Earth."*

The Kansas City Star
August 3, 2004

The Ties that Strengthen

Elderly patients being treated for depression were found to be more functional on daily tasks when they had a large social network, frequent social contacts, and the perception that they had social support. They were also less likely to become more seriously depressed.

Science and Spirit

More formally, some people find understanding and comfort in support groups with others who have similar problems. In whatever way individuals get help, the experience of overcoming stress helps them develop resilience and self-reliance.

Learning to be Resilient

We will learn to be resilient when we do not let momentary setbacks keep us from believing in our abilities. Our determination must be so intense that nothing can stop us. Every time we face a difficult situation and overcome it, we become strengthened and more self-reliant by our success. This process is similar to what happens when we build our muscles with weight training. We lift a weight heavy enough to cause stress in the muscle, which then rebuilds and strengthens. When we are building physical stamina, we likewise stress ourselves just a little by going farther than is comfortable. Our body adapts gradually and is able to do more work.

So, too, we build our character by challenging ourselves, developing new coping skills, and persisting until we reach a new level of resilience. We do this in our work and our social and recreational lives. Challenges make life exciting and help us to grow.

Sometimes, however, we are faced with catastrophic events which may threaten to overwhelm our ability to cope. We could, then, fall back on our social support networks to help us through. We may search out the facts of the situation and look for advice from experts. At other times, however, we simply get used to a certain set of events that at first we experienced as overwhelming.

As a direct result of the terrorist attacks on September 11, 2001, which destroyed the World Trade Center in New York City, many people were initially uneasy or fearful about flying or traveling. However, in time, most learned to accept as a necessity the tight security checks at the airport, the long waits, and the armed security patrols. Time was taken to collect facts, evaluate risks, and talk about the situation with others. As a result, people were no longer as distressed. On the surface, at least, life appeared to return to normal even though drastic changes had taken place in their sense of security and their lives. They took comfort in Anne Morrow Lindbergh's thought that "only in growth, reform and change…is true security to be found."

Perseverance Creates Resilience

We admire, honor, and respect people who survive a major hardship such as war, famine, or economic bad times. However, we also recognize that resilience and perseverance are the stuff of everyday life. We can even turn chronic problems into conditions which are tolerable.

Here is the story of an ordinary man who awoke recently to the debilitating pain of chronic sciatica.

Let the day begin

As I lay awake, I felt even before I moved that this would be a difficult day. My back felt "delicate." Sure enough, as soon as I began to roll my legs over the side of the bed the pains shot down my leg like an electric charge. I lay flat. Should I just stay in bed? It was still early and the gentle breathing of my wife beside me made that option a comforting one. Getting out of bed, getting dressed, getting into the car, suffering through the pain at the gym - when did all those normal daily routines become challenges? I didn't know myself anymore.

Round One

Still, I enjoy my life. I don't want to be an invalid. I have things to do and places to go. So, I get up gingerly, and limp and wince my way through my morning routine. Where is my long-handled shoe horn? How can I get my feet into my trousers and pull them up without moaning too loudly and waking up my wife? I think of my office. I love my office - the broad desk waiting with my projects; the souvenirs of my work and life and friends and family. It IS my life and I belong there. I can work through this pain. I'll feel better after some stretching.

I felt even before I moved that this would be a difficult day.

CHAPTER **2**

Bee Persistent

"When you feel that being persistent is a difficult task, think of the bee. A red clover blossom contains less than one eighth of a grain of sugar; 7,000 grains are required to make a pound of honey. A bee, flitting here and there for sweetness, must visit 56,000 clover heads for a pound of honey: and there are about sixty flower tubes to each clover head. When a bee performs that operation 60 times 56,000 or 3,360,000 times, it secures enough sweetness for only one pound of honey!"

Rolf B. White, ed.
The Great Business Quotations

Round Two

I make it to the car, grateful that I traded in my little Miata for the sedate sedan. The little sports car was a real ego boost when I turned fifty, but now I am happy to settle for comfort. I arrive at the gym feeling a little self-conscious when all the buff energetic early-risers bounce past me on the way to their workouts. I try to walk without seeming too obviously in pain. I do a few stretches, breathing through the excruciating pain. Stop, breathe, stretch, walk. Breathe again.

Come on, one more lap, I urge my body. You can do this. I make it around the track, this time with more spring in my steps and a smoother gait. Why is this so difficult? I think of my colleague again - his face shining with eagerness about our project. I can't let him down. I don't want to let myself down. Talking and breathing my way through the pain I find myself feeling better. I'm still standing and the bell rings the end of round two.

Round Three

I shower and manage to dry my feet without losing my balance. The trousers are more willing to slide up my legs and settle around my waist. If I walk carefully and don't jar my back I can manage to at least look pain-free. Things are getting easier. I am still in pain, but I know I can do this. I drive to the office. Park. Ride up in the elevator. Yes!! I am here and smiling! My day begins. The pain is not down for the count, but I declare myself the winner anyway.

Giacomo Spero

And the Winner Is...You

This scenario is repeated over and over again, by people young and old, "healthy" or disabled. For many, suffering is a part of living. We can sit down in a puddle and moan about it, or we can get up, brush ourselves off, and cope with life. Pain is real and sometimes inevitable. It is often said that there is no growth without pain! When we are motivated and determined, we can find a way to carry on a rewarding life no matter what the circumstances.

So, when are you a winner? We win when we are able to see the joy in life regardless of the situation we find ourselves in. When we are able to cope with adversity, we build the endurance that enables us to appreciate life in its fullness.

You can have anything you want if you want it desperately enough. You must want it with an exuberance that erupts through the skin and joins the energy that created the world.
Sheila Graham

I declare myself the winner.

TIME FOR REFLECTION

One Step at a Time

Think of a time in your life when you were able to reach your goal by breaking the task down into small easy steps.

Idealize the Real

Think of a time in your life when you "idealized the real."

Were you able to create a meaningful life for yourself under these circumstances?

Think of a task you did not want to do but which became fun when you changed your attitude about it.

Encouragement Feeds Determination

Think of someone in your life whose encouragement fed your determination to persevere.

Building Resilience to Stress

What strategies have you used to build resilience?

Overcoming Momentary Setbacks

Describe a time when you were able to overcome a setback because you were intensely determined to succeed.

The Einstein Difference

"Asked how he was different from the average person, Einstein replied that the average person would stop when he found the needle in the haystack. He, however, would tear the entire haystack apart looking for all the possible needles."

Adapted from
Michael Michalk

Someone Who Inspires Me

Here is space to tell the story of someone whose resilience and determination have been an inspiration to you.

_____

_____

_____

_____

_____

_____

_____

_____

Looking Fear in the Face

"You gain strength, courage, and confidence by every experience in which you really stop to look fear in the face. You are able to say to yourself, 'I lived through this horror. I can take the next thing that comes along.'…You must do the thing you think you cannot do."

Eleanor Roosevelt

CHANGE AND ITS UNFORESEEN CONSEQUENCES

In all phases of human life
and in all forms of life on the planet,
change is inevitable.

Where There is Change, There is Life

In all phases of human life and in all forms of life on the planet, change is inevitable. One of the great advantages of the human race is the amazing ability to adapt; those who can adapt to change, thrive.

	1900	**2000**
• The population of the United States	76 million	250 million
• The value of a 1900 dollar	$1.00	4.5 cents
• Transportation	horse, train	car, plane
• Communication	telegraph	cell phone
• Business transactions	pen, ink, paper	fax, e-mail
• Photographs	daguerreotype	digital
• Letter writing	typewriter	laptop

Most of these changes occurred gradually enough for us to accept over time. However, in the past 25 years, technological advances have accelerated to such an extent that some people have to make tremendous efforts in order to keep up. Each generation is subjected to different degrees of pressure. Those born before the 1950s often struggle to adapt, while those born in the 70s and 80s seem to take the rapid change in stride and adapt more easily.

"...for a conscious being, to exist is to change, to change is to mature, to mature is to go on creating oneself endlessly."

Henri Bergson
Nobel Prize in Philosophy, 1927

Some examples of recent events or technologies that will affect us for years to come include:

- Cell phones which send pictures, show movies, e-mail
- Fuel cell technology
- Biotechnology
- Global terrorism
- Outsourcing of customer services jobs to other countries

These are only a few of the events and advances which will alter our lives in unforeseen ways. What will be the consequences unleashed by these events? Can we adapt, or will we be left behind?

Can we adapt, or will we be left behind?

Change Without Opportunity

Sometimes we do not have a choice about change. There can be gradual and benign changes in a society that leave certain people out. Much of the Third World has been left out of the current changes in the modern world. In underprivileged societies, young people who manage to go beyond grade school may still end up doing mind-numbing work that is usually poorly paid.

In our own time and society, many people, through no fault of their own, are being left out of the technological revolution because they can't afford technological tools, or they can't understand how to use them. When changes as substantial as the technological revolution occur, tension and frustration can escalate. Eric Hoffer contends that when the lack of opportunity becomes extreme, uprisings and even revolutions are the likely consequences.

In this chapter, we focus on three ways to face change: coping with change, passively dealing with change, and creating change.

Coping With Change

Seeing change as an opportunity.

Most of us feel more secure when things remain unchanged. To be able to embrace change we need to understand the magnitude of the event and the amount of emotional and physical resources we have available to meet it. In the deadly earthquake which destroyed old San Francisco, a new city was built by the collective effort, aspirations, and vision of people who turned a disaster into a vibrant new city.

Through necessity, a tide of enthusiasm can create radical change in a short time. For example, in World War II as the men went off to war, women stepped into jobs usually reserved for men. As women rose to meet the challenges of the country's war time needs, their aspirations and expectations of what they could offer were changed forever.

In our own lives, we can view the changes that circumstances force upon us as opportunities. For example, a number of the people laid off work in the late 90s were able to forge new careers with long-term opportunities. Most of us, when faced with circumstances which impose change, are driven by our survival instincts into new avenues which we would otherwise never have explored. These days, when people in their sixties are often still considered young, it is curiosity and passion for life that prods retirees into starting new careers, beginning new relationships, and moving to new locations.

Seeking a new beginning.

Sometimes the change forced upon us seems overwhelming. Grave political and economic changes can lead people, out of desperation, to make the wrenching decision to leave their country of origin in search of better opportunities for themselves and their families. The United States was founded on the inspiration and perspiration of such courageous immigrants.

Rose Stolowy's parents, who emigrated from Poland to the United States in 1922, are one example of such immigrants. Here she recalls her excitement about the move:

Change Without Opportunity

"We are usually told that revolutions are set in motion to realize radical changes. Actually, it is drastic change which sets the stage for revolution. Where things have not changed at all, there is the least likelihood of revolution."

Eric Hoffer
Philosopher of the 1960s

When I was 10 years old, the most exciting thing that happened to me was to travel across Europe and come to what they told me was the Golden Land. Coming to this wonderful land was when my life really began. For me it really has been the land of opportunity.

For immigrants like Mrs. Stolowy and her family, the risks of such a huge undertaking were insignificant compared with the opportunities and rewards possible. The dynamics of growth brought about by their striving for success creates progress which makes this country great.

Choice of weapons: Determination to overcome.

When the changes are too great, some people may assume their situation is completely lacking in opportunities. Others, in the same situation, manage to retain a vision of hope. One such man was Gordon Parks. In his autobiography, **Choice of Weapons**, he recounts the story of his grandmother saving him from ghetto violence. She said, "Choose your weapons – either the power of the gun or the power of knowledge." Determination, hope, and the appropriate choice of weapons, made a positive difference for this young man growing up in an environment where despair is common. Today, Gordon Parks is known as a renaissance man: photographer, writer, movie producer, director, and leader.

"For you are the bows from which your children as living arrows are sent forth."

Kahil Gibran

Dealing with loss.

The most difficult change any of us have to face is the loss of a loved one. When change occurs gradually, we unconsciously adapt to the new reality. This is particularly true when our children grow up and leave home. Although most parents are ready, and perhaps eager, to see their children out on their own, some parents live with a longing for the old life of the family. Kahil Gibran writes: *"For you are the bows from which your children as living arrows are sent forth."* For most of us, we are the willing bows and we embrace the flight of our living arrows.

However, when the losses are irrevocable, they can trigger reactions that leave us reeling. With the loss of a loved one, for example, enormous change occurs.

We outwardly adapt to the reality, while we may still be grieving deep inside. We have to cope with all the other adjustments that are necessary.

The biggest challenge of my life was losing my precious family members: my husband, and then 7 months later, my daughter. That was very hard. But you have to accept reality. As you get older, you just feel that you are going to lose the loved ones that you have around you. But it is the cycle of life and you just automatically try to work around it. You have no control over it. Rose Stolowy

Some people, while they carry the memory of their loved one, maintain the inner harmony necessary to survive because they **accept the reality of the cycle of life**.

Passively Dealing with Change

Do we need change?

The desire to maintain the status quo causes some people to fight against change or try to delay the uncertainty that change can bring. But, how are we to evaluate the consequences of change? There are opportunities throughout our lives to embrace a change that may have seemed risky at the time. Sometimes, we may not have been bold enough to take advantage of an opportunity. It may have seemed more rational not to embrace a change. Yet we may later remember that decision with wistfulness and wonder what our lives would have been like had we taken the risk.

The founder of Hallmark Cards, Joyce Hall, sent the following memo to his senior managers: *"Don't be afraid to try something new. But be sure that the new way is not just different, but better."* **It is important to evaluate the consequences of change.**

Must we always say "yes" to change? We may be faced with having to choose between professional acclaim and our own personal satisfaction. Charles Gusewelle, a

For the old, the new is usually bad news.

Eric Hoffer

columnist for the *Kansas City Star*, was once invited to write a syndicated column three days a week. However, it would have meant writing only one column a week of his essays about life that are so meaningful to him and his readers. The other two columns would have been news columns. He declined this opportunity for celebrity. He couldn't "sing his song" in the news columns. Because this great opportunity would have been too high a cost to his creative integrity, he declined.

Ignoring change.

Today, the rapid advances in technology are driving worldwide change. Part of the problem created by this rapid change is the enormous gap, not just between generations, but between people of the same generation. Some are able to integrate their lives with the technological age, while others fail to embrace, or even adapt, to the new tools.

*My husband brought home **another** electronic "toy" today – a digital camera! Okay, so I won't have to use it. But, that is just another one on a laundry list of tech toys I can't use. This house is getting downright scary.*

Have a friend over to watch a video? Nope, I can't get the DVD player to obey my commands. Send an e-mail to my older sister? Nope, not this gal. I prefer snail-mail.

When the electricity goes off, I can't reset the stove-top digital clock. The instructions are written in Japenglish and I don't speak that language. My Lexus has On-Star, but no one has been able to tell me how to get it to work, not even my twenty-year-old honors physics major!

So, what do I think of technology? Does Dante mention a tech Hell? Well, he would have had he lived in the 21st century. I'm just hoping I can move on before I feel like an alien in my own home.
Olivia

Guilty Latecomers

Executives who have delayed becoming computer literate are often getting private tutoring clandestinely, reports Christopher S. Stewart. As the skilled administrators they relied on get laid off, these executives are left having to do some of their own computer work themselves. They fear that if their lack of skills were known they would appear obsolete.

The New York Times
November 2, 2003

Yes, You Can Become Tech Literate, Olivia!

There are a lot of Olivias in the world, along with an equal number of tech phobic men. However, the tech phobic are a slowly dwindling number. People over 50 account for the greatest number of new converts to on-line shopping. There are many programs offered to help people learn the tech skills they need.

There is a certain degree of excitement in being able to understand new technology. When we learn to master the new tools of our time, we challenge our mind and open new ways to connect with the world around us. The conscious effort to bridge the old with the new renews our vitality and "joie de vivre." It links the excitement of the present with the wisdom of the past.

Of course I can use the computer! How do you expect me to keep up with the world if I don't go online? I have a cell phone, too.   Maggie Neff

Costs and benefits of change.

Let's consider the situation of a couple whose children have left home. Should they stay in their large family home or move to a smaller house or condominium? This raises many questions because of the memories and emotional ties to the house. For example:

- What are the emotional benefits and costs of staying in the house?

- Can we deal with sorting through memories and giving things away?

- Can our house be modified to meet our changing physical needs?

- How often do our children and grandchildren visit our home?

- Would there be a financial benefit to living in a smaller place?

- Are we still interested and able to manage our garden?

- Would our new lifestyle be easier without a house?

Some are able to integrate their lives with the technological age, while others fail to embrace, or even adapt to the new tools.

The point of the exercise is to evaluate the consequences of making a change. Will it support our physical, emotional, social, and financial harmony? In the face of changing circumstances, our goal is to foster and maintain a sense of balance and well-being.

Several years after the death of her husband, my mother finally decided to give up her beautiful home and garden when she found herself spending too much time worrying about getting help with the gardening in summer and snow removal in winter.

Although she missed her exquisite garden, a source of great pride and delight, she was relieved to be rid of the worry. She found other activities that brought her joy without the huge responsibility. Her new, smaller home became an outlet for her love of color and design.

S.G. Hope

Maintaining traditions.

If change is part of living, so are traditions. They are links that connect generations and affirm the bonds of a culture. They give us a much-needed sense of identity, continuity, and belonging. In some societies, there are individuals who are considered "living treasures." These are the people who have maintained the rituals or crafts of an earlier time which seem obsolete in the modern world. We are all enriched by such people who sustain our traditions. By keeping the past alive, they help us to have a new perspective on the present. **We can accept change and yet continue to value the traditions which are expressions of our heritage.**

Creating Change

Some people are blessed with a vision which transcends their life. They do not seek change, but create change. They do not imagine what an enormous impact their vision will have on the future.

What Will Become of Your Traditions?

Just because you do not live in a traditional family, does not mean you have to give up traditions. Make up new ones to suit your situation.

"In the years to come, families are more likely to remember the personalities - the aunt who never tired of playing board games, or grandfather who lovingly teased with a twinkle in his eye - rather than the food or a table decoration: It's the people - and the connections that count."

Charlotte Shoup Olsen
Family Systems Specialist

Abraham, the father of the Jewish, Christian, and Moslem faiths, set in motion the unforeseen changes that gave birth to western thought and modern civilization. He believed that God spoke directly to him, a radical departure from the beliefs of the time. From his insight and experiences came the understanding of the value of the individual as an entity distinct within the group.

With the invention of moveable type many centuries later, access to books, and hence knowledge, became a possibility for anyone who was curious and fortunate enough to be able to acquire it. This gave the individual real power to shape his own destiny apart from the wishes of the powerful elite. The access to knowledge open to so many led to an explosion of new ideas, discoveries, and opportunities.

There is always tension between leading innovators and policy makers because the consequences of scientific and technological discoveries cannot be predicted with certainty. Discoveries can create fear in those who cannot accept the risks of change, who feel their beliefs or values are challenged. The controversy over stem cell research is only one example.

But think of the many people who, following their creative urge, change our world in less threatening ways. In April of 2003, *AARP* published an article about *"The Fifty Most Innovative Americans over Fifty."* The editors called innovators gift-givers because their work results in benefits for all of us: people like Jimmy Carter, who works tirelessly for peace; Norma Kamali, a high-fashion designer for working women; Toni Morrison, who brought literature of the black experience into the mainstream; or Dean Kamen, inventor of the Segway scooter for urban transportation and the iBOT wheel chair which can climb stairs.

> *"A butterfly stirring the air today in Peking can transform storm systems next month in New York."*
>
> James Gleick author of *Chaos*

Yes, You Can … Deal Successfully With Change

How can we cope with the changes that inevitably occur? When faced with enough dissatisfaction, we may be forced to take a risk, and try something new.

Planning for Change

- Collect facts about your desired new goal.

- Evaluate the risks.

- Decide how you will deal with the risks.

- Make a commitment to persevere.

- Define the small steps that will help you reach your goal.

- Tackle each step, one at a time, until you succeed.

- Reevaluate the progress you have made.

- Reward yourself for each accomplishment along the way.

"To succeed takes more than intelligence. It takes persistence, focus, and the sort of insight that comes to the well-prepared mind."

AARP, April 2003

Collect facts about your desired new goal.

TIME FOR REFLECTION

Where There Is Change, There Is Life

What is the biggest difference between your life and that of your grandparents?

Choice of Weapons

Think of a time in your life when you were able to see hope in a situation that appeared hopeless to others.

How did you create your own opportunity?

Creating Change

Think of a small discovery in the past which resulted in a big change in society.

What changes would you like to see created in your life?

Tech Literacy

Name a tech tool you have not yet mastered. Write a list of pros and cons about the benefits of learning to master it. Research the resources available to help you become proficient in the use of that tool.

Adapting to Loss

Remember a time in your life when you were faced with a significant loss.

What strategies did you use to cope?

Maintaining Traditions

What traditions have you maintained in your family?

Is there a certain person in your family who is the "keeper" of the family traditions?

To Retire is Boring

"A recent AARP/Roper Report survey found that 80% of baby boomers plan to work at least part-time during their retirement."

Harvard Business Review
March 2004

PHYSICAL WELL-BEING

2

PHYSICAL WELL-BEING

There is a chasm between the attention we pay to

our cars and and the way we maintain our bodies.

A simplistic approach to physical well-being concentrates on building the stamina, strength, balance, and flexibility that make us feel good about our bodies. The importance of cultivating our senses is often overlooked. When we exercise we feel better because we have the energy to do the things we want to do. Yet it is the pleasure we get from exercising that keeps us motivated.

Physical well-being and positive attitude enhance each other. If we have a positive frame of mind we can experience the joy of the natural world around us and we feel that life is good. Likewise, if we exercise, we feel more energetic and alive because energy comes from movement.

When we are young, we seek the exhilaration of an exciting game of tennis, an arduous climbing expedition, or a brisk ten-mile run. These are good moments, but they bring a different kind of experience from the quiet joy of observing the world around us.

As we get older, even though our physical powers begin to diminish, we may become more sensitive and ready to enjoy small pleasures. We take the time to fully appreciate little touches of humor, the pleasure of watching birds building their nests, a soft rain, and the blossoming of new flowers. Because our awareness enriches our life and gives it more meaning, we learn to enjoy life more with less.

> *"Life is not measured by the number of breaths we take, but by the moments that take our breath away."*
>
> George Carlin

My Home By the Sea
by Mary Grant

When I awaken at my home
                 by the sea,

The sound of the surf calls
                 out to me

Like a beckoning siren beyond
                 my reach—

So I roll out of bed and walk
                 down to the beach.

In day's first light it's a
                 lonely scene

But the tide-washed beach
                 is smooth and clean.

In the company of sea gulls
                 I go walking along

Remembering a poem or the
                 words of a song.

It's peace and contentment
                 as I go on my way

Giving thanks once again
                 for another new day.

Mary Grant's poem, "*My Home By the Sea,*" is a lovely example of how the interaction of the mind and the body bring us contentment and joy. Her morning walk sets off her whole day as she opens her senses to the beauty of the world around her.

In the later stage of our relay of life there is an immediacy, an urgency to live in the moment. Life becomes more precious because we realize there is so much we want to enjoy and so little time to enjoy it. The awareness of our own mortality intensifies our experiences. We finally recognize the limits of our physical strength and we become increasingly drawn to spiritual values.

Savor Life

"Life isn't all about business. It's about waking up every morning and feeling grateful that you are about to have another good day."

Loretta LaRoche
Stress-management Consultant

There is so much we want to enjoy

and so little time to enjoy it.

Our sophisticated language capability
conveys only 25% of what we are trying to communicate;
the other 75% is transmitted through our senses.

"When our senses are in balance and harmony, we are blessed with a happy state of mind."

Giacomo Spero

Our senses are the first means by which we interact with the environment. Our sophisticated language capability conveys only 25% of what we are trying to communicate; the other 75% is transmitted through our senses. Our senses are important not just to our physical well-being but to the feeling of being connected with our world.

Cultivating our Senses

Our first experience of the world is sensual. Babies love to be touched and respond to color and sound and smile with contentment. As adults we continue to derive feelings of well-being from our senses. This is particularly true when we have wonderful experiences that are shared with others.

Glenda Spellerberg has spent a great deal of thought creating a beautiful home environment full of good scents, lovely colors, and inviting textures.

I really respond to color, scent and textures. My mom is very colorful as well. Her living room walls are painted ivory with a touch of red. Her dining room is red and natural wood. There is color everywhere, so I am sure I got my love of beauty and color from my mom.

Talking about the warm, beautiful environment of her home led Glenda directly to memories of her loving mother. She demonstrates the direct link between our sensual environment and our emotions and memory.

We cultivate our senses by broadening our awareness and experiences beyond what is familiar to us. It is easy to just "grab a bite" and enjoy our familiar fast and convenient foods. On the other hand, we could try the adventure and delights of savoring Coquilles St. Jacques, chicken paprika, or osso buco.

The Senses Sustain Us

"If I had but two loaves of bread, I would sell one and buy hyacinths, for they would feed my soul."

The Koran

Appreciate Diversity Through the Senses

"God gave us memory so that we might have roses in December."

Anonymous

The senses we choose to refine help us to develop our uniqueness and give us a frame of reference with which to understand our world. A poet attuned to his sensory experiences is able to create poems that stir us. Musicians cultivate the subtleties of melody and rhythm to produce music that moves us. Some composers expand their musical vocabulary by listening to the music of other cultures, and adapting those melodies and rhythms to their own musical heritage.

Modern technology has enabled us to experience sounds and sights that are outside our every day encounters. Movies, television, and the Internet bring sights and sounds of faraway places into our homes and tempt us to visit them in person.

Can we expand our sensory pleasure simply by paying closer attention to what is near at hand? What beautiful sounds or sights are ready to welcome us in our own garden? Can we slow down enough to really pay attention to the bird songs in early spring, the fragrance of a freshly mown lawn, or the tantalizing beauty of autumn leaves? What about a child's radiant smile or the feel of a tender hug?

Cultivating our senses increases our joie de vivre when we learn to enjoy and experience what is near at hand. Sensory memories stay vital as we grow older. Therefore, even with faculties impaired by age, our senses can still contribute much that bring us joy and pleasure.

Dying to be Touched

In the 13th century, Emperor Fredrick II of Germany did an experiment to try to determine the basic language of humankind. He took some babies away from their mothers and gave them to nurses who were forbidden to touch or talk to them. Every baby died before they were old enough to talk. Epitaphs on some of the infants graves read, *"They could not live without petting."*

Phyllis R. Davis, PhD
Psychologist

A Cocktail of the Senses

"Love and touching are two faces of the same thing."

Ashley Montagu, anthropologist

The sense of touch.

All the senses are vital for our well-being. Touch, however, is essential to our survival.

Every culture has evolved rules and expectations about touching which often implies some kind of commitment. The handshake, for example, can mean friendship, commitment, or agreement. At one time, people did not write contracts, they just "shook on it" and looked sincerely into each other's eyes. The handshake made an oral agreement binding. A lot of information is exchanged in a handshake and the glance that accompanies it.

A hug is a silent expression of feelings that sometimes has more meaning than spoken words. It is often used to express friendship and affection. However, a strong tight hug can feel too aggressive. A limp hug can feel like a rejection. How we give and receive hugs will largely depend on the culture in which we live.

Another way we express ourselves through touching is with a kiss. Kissing is not just an expression of romantic feeling; it can also communicate friendship, loyalty, caring and concern, depending on the circumstances. Kissing on the forehead can mean a blessing. In some cultures, kissing can imply that you are part of the family or tribe.

A strong tight hug can feel too aggressive.

The sense of smell.

The close contact that occurs with a hug or a kiss makes it possible for another very important sense to "speak" to us, the sense of smell. From the moment of our birth this sense plays an important role in survival. For example, when an infant is only a few days old it can recognize its mother through its sense of smell. Yet, even more than touch, we are not always aware of the power of smell on our emotions.

Each of us has experienced special aromas that awaken memories and bring us pleasure. Yet we may be unaware of a particular scent until we are swept back in memory to the time we first experienced it. For example, the scent of roses on a summer may evoke memories of a beloved grandmother.

Attar of Roses

Rosa Damascena are special roses cultivated in southern Bulgaria in the valley where the Maritsa river flows. Here there are fields and fields of roses. Once a year, these roses are harvested to create a phenomenal array of products such as attar of roses, rose petal jam and rose water. Although we lived in Egypt, my grandmother was from Bulgaria. Every year at rose harvest time, she would go to the market and come home with a bag of rose petals. I remember her setting up her primitive distilling unit, boiling the petals and condensing the water in tubes. All the neighbors knew that Grandmother Jonathan was doing her yearly rose thing. Every year she created rose water and rose petal jam. When she wanted you to feel good, she made compresses of rose water for your forehead. A big reward was a spoonful of rose petal jam.

Jack

Each of us has experienced special aromas that awaken memories and bring us pleasure.

Good smells bring so much to our daily lives. A cinnamon aroma may make us feel nostalgic because it reminds us of family celebrations. The essence of orange is sometimes used in the air system of nursing homes to help people perk up. Lavender is said to evoke a feeling of calmness. In Egypt, the perfume of jasmine flowers brings so much pleasure that one common greeting is *Sabakh el yasmeene*, "May your morning be full of jasmine."

My mother, who grew up in a desert climate, would get very excited as we drove over the coast mountains to the desert region of British Columbia. She would have her head out of the window waiting for the scent of the sage to tell her she had arrived home.
Sheelagh

The reality is, however, that too much of a good thing can be harmful. A true story from Hallmark Cards in the 60s illustrates that too much of a good thing can make us sick.

Overwhelming the Senses

Hallmark was experimenting with the use of aromas for humorous greetings cards. We tested different smells such as the aroma of barbecue, coffee, and apple pie. These were encapsulated and silk-screened onto the cards. We tested 300 cards of each aroma and they were very successful.

Now we had to fulfill the expectations of our distribution system and produce 60,000 of these aromatic cards. As we went into production, I was called by a panicky supervisor. The workers, while applying the special aroma chips on the cards, were feeling nauseated and were fainting. It was too much of a good thing and had become dangerous. We had to stop production.
Jack

Moderation is important. We can enjoy most things around us if we do so in moderation and we focus on healthy pleasure and on moments of enjoyment.

The sweet scent of aromas are free gifts of joy offered to us every day.

When Odors Talk, Do We Listen?

Research suggests that body odors are a primitive means of communication. They inspire sexual readiness and signal fear and anxiety, among other things. We know that ancient Arab, Roman, and Egyptian cultures tried to manipulate their body odors, in particular through the use of perfumes.

Charles Forelle
The Wall Street Journal
June 16, 2003

The sense of taste.

Taste and smell are intertwined. There are not only cultural influences on taste and smell, there are also social implications. Every nation has the equivalent of the coffeehouse. It is not just the taste and smell of the coffee or cigarettes that draws people to these places. It is also the social atmosphere. People go to drink, smoke, and relax with friends, and in some countries to talk about politics.

What appeals to our sense of taste varies with body chemistry, the culture we grew up in, and the fashion of the time. For example, it used to be that many Americans were satisfied to drink instant coffee or tea. But in the past decade there has been a growing demand for a variety of teas and coffees that would have seemed exotic or foreign before. Many people can now distinguish between Arabica and Columbian coffee. They may have a preference for Italian roast or espresso coffee. Tea drinkers argue the value of whole leaf vs tea bags, or the health benefits of green, black, or herbal teas.

Eating well is one of our greatest pleasures. When we eat slowly and savor the diverse bounty of tastes, textures, and smells of the food available to us from all around the world we enhance our well-being. The true measure of satisfaction from a wonderful meal, however, is the conviviality of sharing the food with others.

Pressong Wittaya, a newspaperman from Bangkok, was my traveling companion during my first two weeks in the United States in 1950. We ate meals together. As the food was served, he would open a silver box from which he would pull one or two half inch long peppers which he cut into small pieces. He would not start eating until he had sprinkled the pepper on his meal. Once, I sampled a little speck on my spoonful of rice. I was shocked at how it burned my palate. I gasped for water while he contentedly savored every morsel. Pressong's sense of taste did not match mine, but I understood his delight in spicy foods as a part of his culture. Jack

---

The Taste of Aromas

"Close your eyes and try to remember the exact bouquet of a skillet in which delicate onions, noble garlic cloves, stoic red peppers, and tender tomatoes are sizzling in olive oil...Sometimes, when I evoke the aroma of a mouthwatering dish, nostalgia and pleasure move me to tears."

Isabelle Allende
Novelist

In some cultures, highly spiced foods are not only a necessity, but, the added ingredient that makes meals satisfying. For Pressong, the spicy pepper was comfort food that helped him feel more at home. For an American in Thailand, it might be a piece of apple pie à la mode or a hamburger smothered in catsup that satisfies his longing for home.

One cannot truly taste food without the stimulation of the sense of smell. Food will taste good if it smells good. Entering into a bakery, the aroma of a freshly baked loaf entices us to sit down, break the crust open, spread it with butter or cheese, and savor the first bite. The combination of aroma, taste, and texture of the bread adds to our pleasure.

There are more books written about food, recipes, and cooking than any other topic except the Bible. Not only does the writing tantalize potential buyers, but the photos themselves evoke, with anticipation, the pleasure of tasting a new recipe. When we take the time to experiment and share our culinary successes with others, life feels abundant.

The sense of hearing.

Just as the pleasures we derive from taste are heavily influenced by our culture, so, too, is the pleasure we derive from music. Melody influences our emotions. In Hungary, the folk music has a lot of minor notes and seems sad to a person from Austria where polkas or waltzes are usually sweet and happy. The close harmonies of the folk choirs in Bulgaria may sound discordant or "primitive" to our American ears. In each generation, a new music is created that helps young people bond together.

In spite of specific differences, it is evident that we all respond in similar ways to particular sounds and rhythms. Who can resist the urge to move when hearing a marching band? Who does not get misty-eyed when their national anthem is played? Who can sit still when the music is dancing?

Taste and smell are intertwined.

There are natural sounds that we can all relate to. Most people find the sound of a waterfall or waves lapping a shore very soothing. The sound of the autumn leaves rustling in the wind or the raucous cicadas in the summer can be comforting. A story by Kermit Long in **Great Business Quotations**, points out that we hear what we listen for.

Two men were walking along a crowded sidewalk in a downtown business area. Suddenly one exclaimed, "Listen to the lovely sound of that cricket." But the other could not hear it. He asked his companion how he could detect the sound of a cricket amid the din of people and traffic. The first man had trained himself to listen to the voice of nature. But he didn't explain. He simply took a coin out of his pocket and dropped it to the sidewalk, whereupon a dozen people began to look about them. "We hear, what we listen for," he said.

Paying attention can help us be aware of what is good and what is harmful. Loud discordant sounds make us shiver. We react with fear to a loud report. The gentle melodious sounds of a mourning dove at dawn can make us feel relaxed and happy. The gurgling of a baby or the deep laugh of our friend brings delight. Sounds, like taste, can be a signal alerting us to whether something is "on" or "off."

The Sound of the Tambourine

When I was in boarding school recovering from an accident I was unable to participate in sports with the other boys. The headmaster used two tambourines to help me improve my eye/hand coordination. These were old-fashioned tambourines that were made with leather stretched over circles of wood and dried in the sun until they became nice and taut.

To play, we would stand 60 feet away from each other and launch a hard ball with the tambourine. If I hit the ball in the sweet spot in the center of the tambourine there was a distinct sound that was quite different from the one produced when I hit it near the rim. The pleasure was to volley back and forth, listening for the beautiful echoing sound of the ball hitting the sweet spot. Jack

Loud discordant sounds make us shiver.

The sense of sight.

"Light is life, it is the eye of the mind."

Giacomo Spero

So much of our lives depends on seeing well and understanding what we see. For many people, sight is the sense that can most easily be conjured in our mind. The sight of the natural world with its green trees, clouds, sun, rain, birds and animals is calming and can promote good health. We can close our eyes and visualize a beautiful sunrise that gives us a feeling of being connected to the whole of life.

Connecting to the Whole of Life

Early one morning, standing high over the water on the cliffs of Nazare, Portugal, I watched a fishing crew put their boat out to sea. This lonely boat, bobbing on the big waves was getting smaller and smaller as it sailed toward the horizon. Soon, it was only a little speck against the immensity of the sea. I was all alone except for the soaring birds. The sun's first rays falling on the shimmering sea heightened my feelings. I felt so small in comparison to the vastness of the ocean.

"Lord be by my side. The sea is so big and my boat is so small."   Jack

We have talked about these senses as if they are separate, but of course, when we see the golden rays of the sunrise reflecting across the ocean, we also hear the waves lapping the shore. We feel the touch of the wind on our face and smell the salty air. In moments like these, when our senses come together like the instruments in an orchestra, we are inspired and humbled by the immensity of what we experience.

Our bodies are made to connect to the world through our senses. The changes that occur, as a result of what we perceive, create emotions, which in turn result in feelings that modify the way we think and act.

"Contemplating beautiful objects puts us in a good mood... or what brain scientists describe as a 'state of positive affect.'"

Steven Johnson
Journalist

"Look to this day!
for it is life.
The very Life of life.
For yesterday is
already a dream
and tomorrow is only a
vision: But today, well
lived, makes every
yesterday a dream of
happiness, and every
tomorrow a vision
of hope."

Attributed to Kalidasa (#419)

The following story dramatically illustrates how the pleasure of our senses can directly affect our physical well-being.

The Far Horizon

My husband had had open heart surgery two months before we arrived at our summer place on the island. He said he was not sure he wanted to live because the pain in his chest was so bad. Several days after we settled into our house, his son asked him if he wanted to go to the beach. My husband hesitated, but finally agreed he could manage it.

We drove in silence the short distance to the saltwater pond that bordered on the sea. For a moment, we sat on a log and looked out across the pond to the sea that stretched out to the horizon. After awhile, my husband got up and walked slowly down the beach. We did not follow, sensing that he needed to be alone.

He was gone so long we began to worry. As we were about to go looking for him, he came jauntily around a curve in the beach, waving and smiling. Something about the beach, the vastness of the ocean before him, the sun, the birds circling had given my husband the connection to life he needed. The decision was made. He lived for nine more joyful years.

S.G. Hope

Sights, sounds, smells, tastes, and touch can not only create a feeling of well-being, but also help us to thrive and restore us to health. Our bodies are made to connect to the world through our senses. The feelings that occur when we are totally aware of our environment inspire us to live more fully.

All Together Now

In the evening, as I walked along the boardwalk at the edge of Nazare, my nose followed the delicious aroma of freshly grilling sardines. I arrived at a primitive kitchen with an open charcoal grill. There, a Portuguese man and wife with weathered faces, greeted me with smiling eyes. I pointed to the grill. The woman beckoned me to a small wooden table under the grape vine covered pergola, surrounded by colorful flowers. Small, black olives glistening with olive oil arrived at the table. The fragrances of the sardines and freshly baked bread raised my expectations. Finally, the black olives were joined by crusty peasant bread, grilled sardines, and a light, local beer. All my senses were engaged in this meal. I slowly savored every mouthful as I watched the last rays of the sun set below the horizon. Lulled by the gentle lapping of the waves, I felt a deep sense of contentment and peace settle over me. Jack

Special moments like these are further enhanced when we are able to share them with others. A beautiful, delicious meal eaten in good company is a feast for all the senses and gives us the greatest feeling of satisfaction. A shared meal becomes a pleasure instead of just a necessity, and the memories we store up are there to sustain us later when we are alone.

Table for One

Despite the fact that eating with others feels good and is better for us, only 54% of Americans eat a meal with their families most days. In fact, one in four people surveyed ate on the run at least a few days a week. "Every day or most days" 46% of Americans eat alone compared with only 25% of Italians.

Sandra Yin

PAUSE FOR REFLECTION

Cultivating the Senses

What senses would you like to broaden and refine at this time in your life?

What steps could you take to cultivate them?

Your Sense of Touch

How do you meet your need for touch every day?

Your Sense of Smell

Write about an aroma which brings back a special moment in your life.

List the aromas which help make your daily life a pleasure.

Your Sense of Taste

What tastes help get your day off to a good start?

Your Sense of Hearing

Think of the sounds in your life that send a shiver of pleasure through your body.

Think of the sounds that comfort you every day.

We expand our sensory pleasure simply by paying closer attention to what is near at hand.

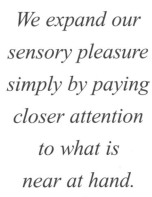

Your Sense of Sight

Describe a sight that brings you a sense of tranquility.

All Together Now

Write down a sensory treasure which played a decisive role in your life.

Physical Well-Being

What are the sensory pleasures that enhanced your well-being today?

Meaningful Conversation

Write about the last time you had a meaningful conversation with friends.

It is time to log out of our chat room, put our computer to sleep,

turn off the TV and invite the gang over.

Let's reclaim our delight in talking to each other,

intimately, over a good meal, in a beautiful setting.

It is extremely important to maintain a positive attitude.

"It should be the function of medicine to help people die young as late in life as possible."

Dr. Ernest Wynder

The mind and body are as interdependent as the hardware and software of the computer. The body could be compared to the hardware, which is the structure, and the mind to the software, which determines how things run. In fact, the body can exist without a conscious mind. A person in a coma is not regarded as really living, but simply alive. The brain relies on the body to provide its fuel, oxygen rich blood. The body relies on the brain to make the decisions necessary to sustain a meaningful life. This helps us not just to live, but to thrive. *Mens sana in corpore sano*: **"What supports a healthy body is also essential for a healthy mind."**

Personal trainer Tina Sprinkle talked about the importance of balancing mind and body in this way:

The commitment to exercise does not just stop with the body. To me it is a whole thing. We don't separate the physical from the intellectual; the spiritual from the emotional. We are holistic beings. I am as proactive in my life about learning as I am about physical fitness.

Bill Neaves, director of the Stowers Institute for Medical Research, was asked about the importance of physical well-being in creating emotional well-being. In general, he feels that for most of us good health is important to a positive attitude. He himself has a commitment to regular exercise and a healthy diet and looks young and fit.

Dr. Neaves is personally acquainted with two remarkable men who, although paralyzed, have not been mentally or emotionally compromised. After talking with admiration about the late Christopher Reeves, who had a spinal cord injury, and Stephen Hawking who suffers from ALS, Dr. Neaves added this insightful observation: **"Being in sufficiently good health to be unaware of one's body as a restraining influence, is extremely important to maintaining a positive attitude."**

A Frazzled Mind, A Weakened Body

Research has shown that the body is harmed by stresses which are ongoing. One of the stress hormones, cortisol in particular, can weaken the immune system and is implicated in diseases as diverse as osteoporosis and cancer.

"Cure the mind, and you might just help save the body."

David Bjerklie
Reporter, New York

Physicians have long understood the relationship of a balanced, harmonious life to physical well-being and health. The human mind and body are the most beautifully engineered piece of creation. When all is functioning well, every part interacts in balance with each other.

Life Span or Health Span?

"Wish not so much to live long as to live well."

Benjamin Franklin

Our mind, when properly stimulated, continues to develop new neural pathways. On the other hand, the body does not, for the most part, develop new structures. If we focus on healthy living, we can provide our brain with the stimulating environment it needs to continue to grow, and we can help our body to maintain its condition with a minimum of decline. The result would be to extend our health span and thus our quality of life.

We hear about the possibility of extending our life span to as much as 120 years. However, some medical researchers suggest that "efforts to slow aging should not be the mere extension of life but should be to prolong the duration of a **healthy life**. The "good life" depends not on how long we live, but on **how long we live well**. When we are in good health and maintain our mind and body in top condition, the normal deterioration of aging does not cause major changes in our ability to function until our last few years. We deal with these changes best when we accept our body's limitations and learn how to modify or adjust our lifestyle to enhance our physical well-being.

Despite the media focus on health and fitness, we seem to concentrate mainly on reacting to illness rather than on maintaining good health. Yet, even middle-aged people who understand the benefits of appropriate diet and exercise, and then begin a supervised health and fitness routine, can become stronger and may have even more endurance than they did when they were younger.

Even if we begin an exercise program very late in life, we can regain some of the flexibility and strength that has been lost through inactivity.

Astonishingly, even if we begin an exercise program very late in life, we can regain some of the flexibility and strength that has been lost through inactivity. Also, if we adopt a healthy diet we can often reverse damage done by previous bad habits.

Our lives could be more fulfilling if we focus not on extending our life span, but on prolonging our health and fitness span.

Maintaining Good Health

"Look to your health ... for health is a blessing

that money can't buy."

Izaak Walton

Both the mind and body thrive on the same things: access to a stimulating environment, an active physical life, a healthy diet, satisfying relationships, rest and relaxation. These key ingredients provide the means necessary not only to sustain a healthy life, but to **regenerate** our minds and bodies. Those who do not actively seek out these conditions of healthy living will increase their risk of disease.

Before the age of modern medical technology, doctors dealing with illness or accident relied heavily on the natural recuperative powers of the body. Protect, support, and wait and see was a common medical practice. This often worked well when the dysfunction was recognized early and could be corrected with rest, good diet, and moderate exercise. However, today we understand that ignoring medical problems can lead to serious chronic or acute illnesses that may require more intrusive interventions.

Ignoring medical problems can lead to illness that may require more intrusive interventions.

Our first line of defense against disease is an understanding of how our own body functions.

Heed early warnings.

Preventive care is less costly in terms of dollars, time, and stress than trying to deal with a major illness and its consequences. Our first line of defense against disease is an understanding of how our own body functions. This self- knowledge is crucial to early detection and diagnosis. But are we paying attention? Do we wait until the situation becomes unbearable?

Maintain a personal history.

Part of a responsible health discipline is to maintain a personal medical history which can be compiled by getting an annual health exam. This should include a blood chemistry profile, a bone density test, blood pressure check, Body Mass Index, urinalysis, and any other tests our physician decides are necessary. Keeping a running record of the results of these tests will be critical to the health decisions that we make with our healthcare providers.

Update family medical history.

We also need to have an update of our family medical history. Modern science, through DNA research, has added another tool to the diagnostic tests which can help us anticipate problems arising from the hereditary misexpression of our genes. The hope is that, caught in time, some genetic diseases might be arrested or their consequences diverted before they overwhelm us. When we know what genetic disorders we may have inherited, or when we pay attention to the illnesses common in our family, we can be proactive in our choice of lifestyle and prevent or avoid the diseases.

Avoid health risks.

Maintaining good health also means avoiding health risks such as smoking, overindulging in food or alcohol, and physical risk-taking. Furthermore, it is critical for us to attend to our basic needs such as rest, recreation, warmth, proper food, and water. Sometimes we set aside our basic needs because of social pressures or the time constraints of our busy lives. Sir Winston Churchill once commented that many international conferences resulted in poor decisions because some of the delegates failed to use the toilet before entering the conference.

If we heed our body's signals, we not only attend to our physical needs, but also avoid environmental dangers. For example, we need to protect our hearing, as well as our overall health, from continuous loud or unpleasant noises. We need to rest when we are tired. We need to move when we feel physical tension. It is true we can continue to function if we ignore our physical needs, but we may damage our ability to function in a harmonious way. Continuous loud noise can damage our hearing; ignoring our need to rest can lead to sleep disorders; losing touch with our need to move can result in a sedentary lifestyle that saps our energy.

Enlightened companies, aware of the relationship between a healthy body, reduced stress and increased productivity, now provide their employees with exercise rooms, quiet rooms for resting, and a cafeteria that provides healthy food.

When asked where she learned about the importance of maintaining a healthy lifestyle, Glenda gave the credit to her former company.

American Century is a great company for supporting people's health with the different types of programs they have: an in-house gym, aerobics classes after work, opportunities to get a massage, and sometimes classes on good health and eating right. Every year you can have a blood screening. All of that, with the company supporting good health, really had a lot to do with me wanting to be healthy.

An older person can look "delicate" and still maintain flexibility and vigor in mind and body.

Attributes of a Well-Maintained Mind and Body

A legend in the field of athletics, Jesse Owens reached his highest level of performance as a track star because he knew the importance of maintaining a positive attitude and the harmony necessary to create balance, strength, endurance, and flexibility. He was able to integrate these four basic attributes to achieve peak performance.

But it is not only top athletes who need to maintain their mind and body. Use it or lose it applies to everyone. When she works with her clients, Tina Sprinkle, a personal trainer, helps them develop all four aspects of physical well-being with special emphasis on flexibility.

Where I see the imperceptible fading away of physical ability in people as we age is in the area of flexibility. Part of the aging process is not just that we lose muscle mass, but we also lose our ability to bend and stretch due to a drying up of our connective tissue. If we don't intervene with exercise, our body can actually become immobilized from weak muscles and inflexibility.

The dryness, which gradually occurs as we age, causes us to shrink. Age and vigor are not necessarily exclusive of each other. An older person can look "delicate" and still maintain flexibility and vigor in mind and body. A ballerina en pointe may look delicate but has hidden strength. Delicacy with flexibility and the vigor of resilience are often the hallmarks of a well- maintained body and mind in our older years.

The Benefits of Moving

"Stiff and unbending is the principle of Death.

Gentle and yielding is the principle of Life."

Lao Tsu, founder of Taoism

The ancient art of Tai Chi has been found by western researchers to provide many benefits. Writing in *Arthritis Today*, Donna Rae Siegfried listed the following advantages of practicing this gentle, slow discipline.

Tai Chi Improves	Tai Chi Reduces
Flexibility and balance	Stress
Strength	Depression
Circulation	Blood pressure
Immune system	Breathing
Posture	Heart rate
Ability to relax	Pain
Concentration and memory	Inflammation
Mental outlook	

Activity Brings Recovery

"Activity is very important for all of us, whether or not we are disabled...

I was told that any recovery I might make would happen in the first year. But my recovery began five years later and was due to my rigorous exercise program.

By January 2001, I was spending as much as four hours per day on physical therapy."

Christopher Reeve
Actor

Tai Chi is one of many types of exercise we can do even if we no longer are as strong and vigorous as we were in our youth.

Maintaining the Body

Our bodies are designed to work their best when they move and have some physical challenge. Exercise is a natural way to help the body and mind release tension and channel it in a positive direction. Furthermore, when we exercise we increase our energy and zest for living.

If we maintain our body in good health, it should function smoothly well into our 60s, 70s and beyond. The gradual decline is not as great as common wisdom supposes. Our body is remarkably forgiving and resilient, so even if we have "let ourselves go" it is never too late to restore, and even improve upon, our fitness level.

We need to be realistic about what we can and cannot do given our age, level of fitness, and handicaps. All areas of fitness can be worked on, but at an appropriate pace. For example, it might be wiser in our later years to get aerobic exercise on a stationary bike instead of jogging. We need to be discerning about how much we can and should test the limits of our physical endurance.

It would be wise to seek the guidance of experts when trying to get started on a plan for long-term fitness. We may need to seek help from an exercise coach, dietician, physical therapist, or massage therapist.

To maintain our fitness, we could join a class or fitness program. However, all that we may need is the support of someone who has the same drive and determination to achieve peak performance and health. The buddy system is a great help in making lifestyle changes that last.

It will take a month or two before the results of a new fitness regimen will be felt. We will experience an increase in energy before we see any changes in the mirror. But the

It is never too late to restore, and even improve upon, our fitness level.

increased feeling of well-being will become the driving force to help us keep our commitment to exercise. Then exercise will begin to feel not so much like a discipline, but a sensory pleasure. Vicki Franklin, for example, attributes her fitness partly to the fact that she just loves to move.

I say that life is like a dance because I love dance and I know that it's important to move. You dance to different music and you adapt to those different beats. Just like in life. That is who I really am. I like to move. But I also like swimming because of the feeling of synchrony of all the parts of the body working together.

Physical exercise is another important factor in the maintenance of a healthy brain.

Maintaining the Brain

The brain, like the body, thrives on being challenged. In fact, the brain is even more resilient than the body. Stimulating our brains with a rich sensory environment helps strengthen and renew neural connections as well as increase neural capacity. Mentally active individuals in their late eighties and nineties have brains which continue to be flexible and resilient.

It is true that around age 30, our memory for details diminishes in favor of a more global memory: a memory for patterns and concepts. The advantage of this change in memory function is that we may become more creative and able to deal better with complexity, abstraction, and subtlety.

Memory span and the rate at which information is processed decreases with age. However, individuals who continue to stimulate and challenge their minds do not necessarily experience significant decline in normal functioning. In fact, a study by the National Institute on Aging found that 26% of older adults who got memory training showed improvement in their memory capacity that lasted at least two years.

Physical exercise is another important factor in maintaining a healthy brain. When we exercise, blood flow increases so that there is more oxygen for brain tissues. Exercise releases hormones that balance our moods and help us sleep soundly. Finally, exercise can stimulate the chemicals that increase brain function. One study showed that people who had previously been sedentary improved their short-term memory, ability to plan, and concentration when they began a program of walking briskly three days a week.

Stimulating the senses and getting enough exercise engage the brain and make us glad to be alive.

Exercise: The One Best Thing

Whether we are trying to beat cancer, keep our bones strong, get heart healthy, lower our risk of diabetes, overcome depression, or keep our memory sharp and our mind alert, exercise is the remedy that shows up on all the research findings as the best way to maintain our mind and body. **If we do only one thing to improve our physical and mental health, let it be to exercise 30 minutes five days a week.** Then, when we are challenged, we will have the inner strength and resources to overcome difficult situations.

Controlled Tension

As the high jumper waits to begin his jump, he watches as the bar is raised one more notch. Instinctively he relaxes his whole body. Then, packing his muscles, he takes off, pacing his stride. He reaches the jump-off point all coiled like a steel spring and gracefully arches over the bar almost effortlessly.

Had the jumper tensed his muscles while waiting, he would be trying too hard. Too much tension causes our body or mind to falter in some way.

One way to help our body and mind maintain an optimum degree of **controlled tension** is to vary activities. These days, it is common for athletes to cross train to give all the muscles a work out and a rest. We do this in other ways as well. For example, if we engage in intellectual pursuits all day, we may find rest in strenuous physical activity in the evening. A person who is with people all day, may find relaxation in listening to music.

Rest: A Pause That Refreshes

Modern man must learn to break the tensions of daily living or the tensions will break him.

Wilfred A. Peterson

More Power to the Nap

There is a group in Portugal called the Friends of the Siesta whose mission is to *"spread and promote the practice of sleeping siestas as a restful pause…"* The group is trying to defend the tradition of the siesta against the pace of modern life, feeling it improves the quality of life.

Reported in
Science and Spirit
July/August 2003

The constant acceleration of the pace of our daily lives, and information overload, cause conflict between our need for rest and the mounting pressures of keeping up and surviving in today's complex world. All endeavors in life, whether physical, mental, or social, require that we pause if we are to be in top form and not create an imbalance. That pause could be as simple as looking out of a window to change our focus when working at the computer, or it could be taking a 20 minute break after a very intense meeting.

We may also wish to take time out to **relax our mind and body** by having a massage, or by engaging in yoga or Tai Chi. We may learn deep body relaxation or meditation. These skills are not hard to learn. But like everything else, it is the discipline and consistency with which we practice these arts that benefit us the most.

If this is not for you, take heart. Recent studies demonstrate the value of a 20 or 30 minute **nap** in the afternoon. In fact, it is common in many hot countries for businesses to shut down for a couple of hours at noon while everyone goes home for rest and relaxation.

Finally, there is the matter of getting enough **sleep**. Articles in popular magazines have lists of tips on how to get a good night's sleep. Sleeping, a natural function of all animals, is problematic in western culture. We seem to be too busy or unwilling to moderate our activities and live a balanced life. Although some people may do well on only five hours of sleep, the conventional wisdom is that we need eight hours of restful sleep every night.

Of course, the amount of sleep we need for optimum health depends on our unique body type and lifestyle. If we are getting the right amount of sleep for our body and mind, we will feel alert yet rested, calm yet ready for action, emotionally more stable, and less prone to errors in judgment.

There are compelling data that too little sleep can be harmful to our hearts, undermine our immune system, and lead to emotional instability. Taking care of our needs for rest and relaxation during the day increases our chances of giving ourselves the gift of peaceful sleep at night.

Knit Up The 'Raveled Sleeve of Care'

Are your bad sleep habits unraveling you? Here are some hints on getting your sleep life knitted back together.

- **Establish a regular bedtime and routine**

- **Avoid caffeine in the afternoon**

- **Avoid nicotine**

- **Limit alcohol**

- **Get regular exercise**

- **Don't read, work or watch TV in bed**

- **Avoid large evening meals, or meals heavy with grease or spices**

- **Make your bedroom dark, cool, and quiet.**

Donnica L. Moore, M.D.

The value of a 20 minute nap.

Eating Habits

"To lengthen thy life, lessen thy meals."

Benjamin Franklin

The issue of diet continues to be controversial. What is the correct diet for physical well-being? The anti-aging advocates recommend a very low caloric intake because it has been shown to increase the life span in mice. However, in humans it may result in adverse symptoms such as low body temperature and agitation. Some experts suggest that a vegetarian diet is more healthful, yet in some people this may result in anemia and low energy. There is the ongoing battle of high-protein/low-carbohydrate diets versus moderate-protein/high-carbohydrate diets versus moderation in all things!

How are we to choose? Each of us, knowing ourself, can make the best choices for our body and lifestyle. Our grandmother's philosophy of moderation in all things, and the ancient wisdom of "know yourself" can show us the way. Of course, the most effective way to maintain our weight is to simply **eat half as much**. This way, we may even continue to eat a little of the foods that bring us comfort and pleasure.

Fads in Food Advice

It is hard to choose what is good for our health. Advice on what to eat changes so often. Margarine is better for us than butter; margarine has trans fatty acids and is bad. Eggs are too high in cholesterol; eggs are full of healthful omega fats. Nuts, too have been on a roll. Once they were thought too fatty for our good. Now it has been found that "people who eat nuts regularly cut their risk of heart disease by as much as half, compared with those who rarely or never eat nuts."

From University of California, Berkeley, *Wellness Letter*
Vol. 19, issue 8, May 2003

Calm Energy

The highly conditioned high jumper is in an ideal state of calm energy, a state of high energy, and positive mood. People in this state of energy without mental tension are patient, attentive, and productive. This is an ideal state which is often associated with happiness. One small research study found that a state of calm energy is most common between 10 am and 2 pm.

Robert Thayer, PhD
Psychologist

Choosing a Healthy Lifestyle

"The best way to preserve your wealth

is to secure your health."

Doug Lockwood

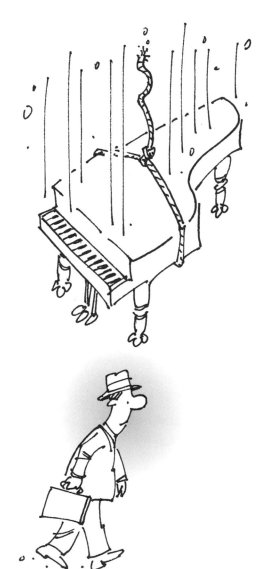

One of the greatest concerns for people nearing retirement age is the fact that just as they will be needing more medical care, the cost of such care is skyrocketing and getting good health insurance can be difficult. More than one study suggests that the Medicare system will become bankrupt. People who are relying on their place of employment for Medigap insurance often find that the coverage is discontinued or is costly to maintain. The reality is that health care costs will take a toll on the financial well-being of baby boomers.

These facts are a reality check. They help underscore the importance of choosing a healthy lifestyle if we want to enjoy not only physical well-being, but financial well-being in our later years.

There is much that happens in our lives over which we have no control. But the body strives to adapt and compensate in order to maintain harmony and balance. What is within our power is to follow a proper diet, exercise regularly, get adequate rest, take part in a social support network, and most importantly, have the desire and determination to feel our best. We have to be patient with steady progress. We have to be understanding of our occasional relapses. Most of all, we must persevere with small steps until finally the changes we make truly become our lifestyle.

Remember, anything is possible if you are determined and make it a priority.

There is much that happens in our lives

over which we have no control.

PAUSE FOR REFLECTION

Life Span or Health Span

Which of these steps are you taking to prolong your health and fitness span?

- Eating a well-balanced diet.
- Controlling my calorie intake.
- Eating a healthy breakfast.
- Exercising regularly.
- Engaging in resistance training with or without weights.
- Engaging in activities that help me maintain good balance.
- Creating balance and harmony in my life.
- Reaching out to a friend for support.
- Getting enough rest.

Maintaining Good Health

What steps have you taken to keep track of your medical history?

What health risks are you conscientious about avoiding?

What basic needs are a priority for you? What are you neglecting?

Determination to Feel Your Best

Think of someone whose determination helped them to overcome illness or disability.

Health Care's Big Bite

A 55 year old who retires in 10 years will need the following amount of money to cover medical expenses as she or he ages:

80 years	$95,000 to $246,000
85 years	$128,000 to $428,000
90 year	$163,000 to $702,000
95 years	$199,000 to $1,137,000

These numbers include premiums for Medigap insurance and Medicare Part B premium.

Janice Revell
Fortune

Attributes of a Well Maintained Mind and Body

How do you maintain your body's flexibility and balance?

Do you know of someone who is flexible and vigorous, yet delicate to look at?

Maintaining Your Brain

Think of the ways your habits help your brain to function well.

In what way is your brain balanced? Flexible?

Maintaining Your Body

What changes could you make to improve your physical fitness?

Rest: The Pause that Refreshes

What types of rest do you enjoy?

Calm Energy

Describe a situation in which you experienced controlled tension.

Eating Habits

What foods and eating habits help you feel your best?

What diminishes your energy?

Choosing a Healthy Lifestyle

What is your strategy for maintaining a healthy lifestyle?

Wash Your Hands!

"Your mother, your teacher, and your doctor all told you to wash your hands. Do you? Probably not. Only 78% of people observed by researchers do. 'Making regular hand washing a lifelong habit would do a lot to curb common infectious diseases,' says the American Society of Microbiology."

Phyllis R. Davis, PhD
Psychologist

3

FINANCIAL WELL-BEING

Build your financial muscle.

"Salud, pesetas, y amor, y tiempo para gozarlos."

This old Spanish proverb outlines the essential ingredients of a good life: health, money, love, and time to enjoy them. It is not enough to know how to stay healthy. It is also important to practice these healthy habits day after day, week after week, year after year. This builds the resilience we need to meet life's challenges. It is also the daily acts of kindness and consideration that build lasting relationships that will sustain us in our later years.

Just as the daily practice of good habits brings balance and harmony in our health and relationships, so, too, the daily attention to how we spend, save, and invest is the basis of our financial well-being. You might wonder if you really need this section:

- **If you are in your twenties** you might think it is mildly interesting. **Read on.** Time is on your side because you have the most to gain from compounding your money.

- **If you are in your thirties**, you might think "Hmm… will this help me budget for a family?" **Read on.** You will discover how living within your income can create a feeling of financial well-being.

- **If you are in your forties**, you may worry about the college expenses your kids will have if they want a good educational start in life. **Read on.** It is late, but not too late to organize your finances for your kids' college.

- **If you are in your fifties**, you may think about your retirement future, but worry that you may outlive your resources. **Read on.** You will want to learn how financial independence can help you live a meaningful life.

Psychological Capital

"Psychological capital melds the idea of financial capital with mental health and well-being. ....A person must withhold psychological resources, saving them for future return. To do this, a person must make the choice to participate in activities that may delay gratification but promise future rewards. So, you add up the components of your life experiences and capital, which make up a value at the end of life when you look back and see what's there."

Mihaly Csikszentmihaliyi, PhD
Psychologist

• **If you are in your sixties**, you may be feeling wistful as you see the enthusiasm of your kids as they start their new lives. **Read on.** You will discover how financial independence allows you, too, to begin a new and meaningful life.

Financial security is to our lifestyle what muscles are to the body. We need to develop our muscles, otherwise we will be limited in our ability to do the things we want to do.

Our financial resources determine our lifestyle; if we have lived only from paycheck to paycheck, we will be at the mercy of events. Do we need to differentiate between our wants and needs? Do we really know how to skillfully develop and manage our financial resources? Finally, have we created a plan to ensure there is harmony among our needs, wants, and financial resources? When we balance our needs with our financial resources, we can enjoy a feeling of abundance, a feeling that we can do what we want to do, when we want to do it, **now and in the future**.

Living on One Income

At the time of our marriage both my wife, Virginia, and I worked. She was a registered nurse training to become an anesthetist; I was beginning my career in the investment business.

We both had a strong desire to raise a family, and we were worried about the consequences of getting accustomed to a lifestyle dependent on two incomes. We felt that if my wife had to reduce her work schedule, we might have trouble adjusting to that smaller income. Because of this possibility, we decided we would live on only my earnings, while saving and investing all of my wife's salary.

This decision proved to be the right one for us. As each of our four children came into our lives, we were not subjected to the emotional shock of being forced to drastically reduce our standard of living.

James E. Stowers

Mr. Stowers' story illustrates how a family structured its resources to support its lifestyle. The Stowers were skillful in balancing their financial priorities to support their essential daily needs while creating a solid financial foundation for their future. With their wants and needs in harmony with their financial resources, the Stowers, were able to live a life which, while fulfilling at the time, also gave them a sense of abundance later in life.

Many of us come into marriage with very different views about financial matters. Money management is one of the most divisive areas of marriage and it is important that couples find a way to agree about how they will manage their money.

Who's the Boss?

When we began our marriage, Bob regarded himself as the "boss," the head of the household, responsible for providing for the family and ensuring that we would not have to depend on others until the day we are put in the ground. From the beginning of our marriage we learned that money was going to be a bit of an issue. Initially, I was the sole wage earner because Bob was in graduate school. Nevertheless, Bob controlled the finances.

After our first child was born, I stayed home, until my frustration with losing control over my use of money became too irritating. The crunch came one day when Bob questioned the amount I had paid for my haircut. "That's it, time to go back to work," I said to myself. The compromise we worked out was that Bob would pay for the "normal bills" and save for the long term, and I would purchase the things that made our lives more comfortable. As the years passed, I began to listen to Bob's advice about savings and IRA's. By the time our sons were in college, we both contributed to the educational costs.

"Do you love life? Then do not squander time, for that's the stuff life is made of."

Benjamin Franklin

Bob commented, "I think you just have to decide if you can both come to an agreement on where you want to be when you stop earning an income."

Although this was never an easy discussion in our marriage, we are pleased with our discipline and agreement which has resulted in us having financial independence and options as we come into retirement age.   Bob and Karen Brush

Each of us will be happier and more successful if we have the discipline to save carefully, control our spending, and manage our money skillfully. If we plan well, we can, like Bob and Karen, and Jim and Virginia, achieve the financial independence that will enable us to enjoy a meaningful life beyond our wage-earning or child-rearing years.

The wisdom of the ages asserts that two things are essential for a meaningful life:

"Enough to live on, and much to live for."

"Since I am known as a "rich" person, I feel I have to tip at least $5 each time I check my coat. On top of that, I would have to wear a very expensive coat, and it would have to be insured. Added up, without a top coat, I save over $20,000 a year."

Aristotle Onassis

PREPARING FOR FINANCIAL INDEPENDENCE

Money is clearly a means to an end

in the marathon of life.

"If you know how to spend less than you get,

you have the philosopher's stone."

Benjamin Franklin

Can we really enjoy a *meaningful life* without being financially secure? It is important not to make earning money an end in itself. Rather, money is simply a means to satisfy our needs and wants. *Financial independence* makes it possible for us to be free to do what we want to do, **when we want to do it**.

Most of us earn our living by working for someone. We exchange our time and skills for financial rewards. Many people long for the day when they will finally have control over how they spend their time. However, unless we understand the true nature of money, and use it wisely, we may not be free to live our lives as we would like.

Money is clearly a means to an end in the marathon of life. I have to have a clear understanding of where my money will come from and how I will spend it. Then, I am going to feel secure and I will be set free to do something that I would not have been able to do...my craft.

Vicki Franklin

When members of a panel were asked "What does retirement mean to you?" time was the one word which consistently came up. Each person's dream relied on having discretion over time. It is striking to us that the most valuable asset we have is the priceless gift of **time**. It cannot be replaced.

Here is a summary of the panel's retirement dreams:

- **Personal freedom**: time to do what I want to do when I want to do it.

- **Relationships**: more time to spend with family and friends.

- **Hobbies, sports**: time for fishing, gardening, golf, quilting.

- **Volunteering**: time to work for my favorite causes.

The Good Life?

An article about consumerism noted that a generation ago, *"the average American family was able to save about 11% of their income."* Today, it takes two working people to be able to supply a family of four with life's basics, which may not include a family vacation, health coverage, and money for a comfortable retirement. *"The American Dream has morphed into a treacherous survival regimen in which the good life is increasingly elusive."*

Bob Herbert
The New York Times

- **Travel**: time to explore the world and its people.

- **Personal writing**: time to write memoirs and research my family tree.

- **Personal growth**: time for personal and spiritual growth.

- **Work**: time to learn and use new skills.

By the age of 60, when we contemplate what we are going to do for the next 30 or more years, **time is our greatest asset**. If we have invested our money for the long term, we will enter the last third of our lives able to enjoy the gift of *time*. Life expectancy is increasing and with it comes the fear of outliving our financial resources. It is easy to "forget" to plan for our retirement. Mr. Stowers once commented:

Time is our greatest asset.

As you travel through life in pursuit of financial independence, you may feel that it is a long journey, full of obstacles. However, after you travel life's road and look back, that same path looks very short. You will wonder how the time could have passed so quickly.

Financial planners remind us that living well into our 90s is a distinct possibility.

Since, for most of us, the possibility is slim that we will inherit sufficient financial resources, it becomes imperative that we plan carefully. We need to understand the nature of money and practice the skills necessary to build the financial resources we need to be self-reliant and enjoy the kind of life we have dreamed of.

Financial Structure Is Necessary For Financial Well-Being

*"I believe that professional management is the most
important contribution to investment success over time."*

James E. Stowers

Everything in life is linked by different elements which are interconnected. Just as a building needs steel girders, cement building blocks, electrical conduits, and other materials to form its structure, so are there elements that make up the building blocks of financial well-being.

There are three key elements which make up our personal financial structure. The **first, is an understanding of the value of money**. Many factors influence the purchasing power of a dollar. Some of these factors are beyond our control, such as the size of the national debt, the trade deficit, and the interest rate charged by the Federal Reserve. These are among the large economic issues that become important during an election year when it is through our political choices that we may make a difference.

The **second** element in our financial structure is something we do have some control over: **investing to take advantage of the compounding of interest**. For example, the value of our assets is dramatically affected by the changing value of a dollar which declines at an average rate of about 5% a year. We can compensate for this by **paying ourselves first** and investing for the long term consistently throughout our life. This will allow us to take advantage of the compounding of interest which will help offset the loss of value of a dollar.

The **final element** in assuring our financial well-being is the **importance of doing a regular financial analysis**. People who live within their means are usually careful to keep close track of their finances, sometimes reviewing their budget every week.

We need to plan carefully so that we can enjoy the kind of life we have dreamed of.

My husband has worked very hard to learn about investing and having money for retirement. Being out of debt has been a big deal to this family. The sense of security is so great not to have a debt over your head or a big credit card bill. If something comes up, you have a little aside to deal with it.   Glenda

Planning for the long-term, however, can seem daunting. Some of us may feel we understand finances well enough to rely on our own informed decisions. Others may want to consult a "financial architect" to help lay out a plan that fits present and future needs. It is sometimes easier to stay focused on long-term goals when we rely on an expert. Whichever way we plan, it is important to be prepared and flexible enough to respond to the many challenges and changes the future will hold.

You may want to consult a "financial architect."

Financial Skills Support Our Financial Structure

In **The Millionaire Next Door**, Thomas J. Stanley wrote, *"Wealth is what you accumulate in assets, not what you make or spend."* In his study, he found that millionaires often live simply. They have a budget and are very aware of how much money they spend even on small items. They have daily as well as lifetime spending goals. **They allow time to plan their financial future.** Their aim is to set themselves free to do what they want in life. Their wants are not only defined by material goods, but also by friendships, joining organizations, and taking part in activities they enjoy.

Planning sets me free. Discipline is a very important part of managing money. Even a small amount of money requires respect. You can make quite a bit of money with a little bit if you hold it, save it, manage it.
Vicki Franklin

When we understand the facts about money, we then must be determined to practice the skills which will make our assets grow. Financial management can be learned early in life and can be refined further through new experiences. Some people seem to have a natural ability to make their money grow over time. For most of us, though, it requires self-discipline, inquiry, study, and sustained effort.

When we think of wealth, we often think it will allow us to buy whatever we want. But in his study on millionaires, Thomas J. Stanley found that, *"The hallmark of the well-adjusted wealthy person is that he lives well below his means. He is truly frugal."* **Financial well-being comes with the security of knowing that we have enough to do what we want to do.**

We will focus on two key skills that can help us build a firm foundation for financial independence: **spending money wisely and investing skillfully**.

Spending Money Wisely

"Beware of little expenses.

A small leak will sink a great ship."

Benjamin Franklin

We will assume that we get our money by working for it; that most of us spend what we earn; and that we may also have credit card debt. Most of us are probably aware that we need to save, but the big question is: **Where will we find the extra money?**

*The hallmark
of the well-adjusted
wealthy person
is that he lives
well below his means.*

When we were in college, my husband and I were living on $200 a month and yet, we had money left over to take a charter flight to visit his family in England every summer. The year we graduated, we were excited at the five-fold increase in our earnings. As we were no longer students we felt justified in spending more money. How disappointed we were to discover that we felt poor and lacking in sufficient resources, even though we had more money to spend. Clearly, it was time to sit down and evaluate our spending habits, set clear savings goals, and make a commitment to each other to stick with the plan.

S.G. Hope

To plan a budget sounds logical. Yet most people find it difficult, especially if they have a lot of fixed debt such as student loans, a mortgage, or credit card debt. The couple quoted above began their financial rehabilitation aware that they did not have:

*Is this something
I really need?*

- **Control over their spending**
- **Clear financial goals**
- **A financial plan**

This awareness is only the first step, though an important one. Some people may easily find ways to cut back on their spending and save money. For many, however, this task seems overwhelming.

We can begin by asking, **"Are we getting our money's worth?"**

One of the most valuable exercises that my wife, Virginia, and I followed, in our effort to improve our financial position, was trying to continually convince ourselves that we were absolutely satisfied with the way we were spending our money. We wanted to get our money's worth. I can't emphasize enough how important this was.

James E. Stowers

It was early in their marriage that Jim and Virginia Stowers took this hard look at their life goals and made a decision to develop a financial plan that would enable them to become financially independent. The key to their plan was to follow a daily discipline of keeping track of every penny they spent. Then, every month, they Stowers looked at their spending record and asked themselves, "Are we getting our money's worth?"

The goal is to continually refine the way we spend our money. Here are some tips on how the Stowers accomplished this important task.

Getting Your Money's Worth

- Keep a daily record of every penny you spend whether it is a cash, check, or credit card purchase. Be specific about the item: eg. list not food but lunch (cafeteria), not utilities but water or electricity.

- Keep your records in one place.

- Categorize your purchases at the end of the week.

- At the end of the month, consolidate your lists and look at your categories. Are they specific enough?

- Look into each category, even at the individual items. Ask yourself, "Did I get my money's worth?"

- Now look over the list again, and ask yourself, "Am I satisfied with the way I am spending my money?" Do you like your spending priorities? If not, go through the list and make a commitment to spend your money in a different way next month. Compare your previous month's spending account with the current one. Were you successful at curbing unnecessary spending?

- Check your savings and investment accounts to evaluate their progress. This will motivate you to stay on course.

Life's Priorities

The simplicity movement has been around for years, but since 9/11, there seems to be a renewed interest in reconsidering the materialistic values of our culture. People use different definitions of simplicity as they reprioritize their lives. *The Trend Letter* says *"many are just asking 'Is this something I really need?' before buying, particularly if the purchase requires going into debt."*

Trend Letter
May 13, 2002

Investing Wisely

> *"Rich people plan for four generations.*
>
> *Poor people plan for Saturday night."*
>
> Gloria Steinem

Every year we delay saving makes the possibility of financial independence much more difficult.

In order to achieve the goal of financial independence, **we must pay ourselves first** so we can have money to trade for something that **will grow in value over time, or will generate income**. We need to start saving enough money as early as possible in order to accumulate enough resources to make meaningful investments and let our money work for us.

I wanted to work for myself, so I had to understand how money makes money. I have a few things I want to do, and that means I have to understand investments and savings and have a clear respect for debt. Accounting gives you a metaphor for life...balances in and out, losses and profits.
Vicki Franklin

One of the first principles of investment is, **"Time is money and money is not nearly as valuable without time."** The earlier we begin to save and invest, the sooner we will be financially independent. Conversely, every year we delay saving makes the possibility of financial independence much more difficult.

Under this principle are two main points. One is that we do better when we save for a long period of time because we can take advantage of compounding. The other is that there is a huge advantage in regular monthly investing.

J. Michael Scarborough, a retirement advisor from Annapolis, Maryland, asserts, *"The new reality for young workers is that somehow, some way, 15 % of their income has to go into retirement savings. Only then will money not be an issue in retirement."*

If we invest every month, regardless of whether the market is up or down, we have a better chance of increasing the value of our investments. This means that even when the market is down, we need to hold on to our investments and continue to put money aside each month.

Current Financial Plans

Are we satisfied with the way we are currently managing our money? Some of us who say "yes" may not be aware of the loss of the value of a dollar over time. For those who say "no" it might open a window of opportunity to an invaluable experience.

Money issues are among the most anxiety provoking topics. When we look with clear eyes at our balance sheet, we face a number of our internal conflicts: between our needs and our wants; between our wants and our means; and between our true values and those we think we have.

To help stimulate our thinking about financial planning, let us answer the following:

- Are we sure we are financially secure for the long-term?

- Are we aware that we can achieve financial independence?

- Does our financial security rely only on Social Security?

- Are we investing or saving enough each month?

- Are we sure that our current strategy will enable us to be financially independent?

- Are we spending too much on life insurance?

- Do we have a plan to provide for ourselves and our dependents if we should become disabled?

Ants or Grasshoppers?

About 75 percent of baby boomers are not confident they will have enough income in retirement. Thirty-six percent report thinking of their finances nearly every day.

On average, surveyed boomers think they will need about $800,000 in savings for retirement and expect they will need it to last as long as 19 years.

Tom Kelly
The Kansas City Star

One of the big pitfalls in planning for our later years is the feeling of comfort we can assume because of social security benefits. Most financial advisors recommend a "three-legged stool" for retirement: Social Security, personal savings and investments, and company retirement income. All of these sources of income require our attention and vigilance. When requested, the government will send an estimate of what our Social Security benefits will be. It may be a surprise to discover how little Social Security will contribute to our future financial well-being.

"The Constitution guarantees you the pursuit of happiness, but it doesn't guarantee to finance the chase."

Anonymous

Social Security

I think the idea of Social Security is important. Though it is not enough to support me and my wife, the idea is good because it provides some security. It needs to be preserved. But I have become accustomed to a standard of living that is in excess of what Social Security could provide. If it hadn't been for my saving of money, we would not be able to live as we do. Saving has been a criteria of our financial planning because I never did put making money as a primary goal of my life.

Stan Friesen, M.D.
Researcher/Author

It may be a surprise to discover how little Social Security will contribute to our future financial well-being.

Importance of Diversified Investments

Mike Dearing did not originally know much about investments, but he knew about the need for financial diversification.

I learned this from an old gentleman named Mr. Spencer. He would come out on the corner every morning and sit on his chair. He used to say, "Always try to get as many incomes as you can from as many places as you can." Diversify, that's what he was saying. Here was this old man, just sitting on the corner, and he was secure.

Mike revealed his four sources of retirement income, all of which were tied to the value of a dollar. When he became aware that all these pensions are sources of fixed income, he decided to invest in mutual growth funds so that his future income would not decrease as the value of a dollar declines.

Acquiring financial management skills and investing are lifelong pursuits. Here are six key strategies that Jim Stowers feels are crucial:

- Buy all the life insurance you need for the least amount of money.

- Start investing as early as possible, and invest as if you will live to be 100 years old.

- Begin investing with the largest sum possible.

- Be determined to save on a regular basis; be disciplined and avoid touching savings.

- Reach for the highest rate of return that feels safe and invest for the long-term.

- Evaluate your progress regularly, and review plans often as conditions change.

The more we know about our financial situation, the better we will be able to channel our resources to meet the ever-changing goals of our needs and dreams.

"Within 10 years, expect the U.S. government to increase the retirement age to 75 to save Social Security from financial ruin and to acknowledge the growing number of active seniors who want to continue working."

Trend Letter
May 13, 2002

We have outlined the structure of our financial future. Yet it is not enough to know all, or some, of these facts. It is when we skillfully put them to work that we will benefit the most. Too often we put off this task. Yet, our current and future well-being depends so much on our determination to plan and manage our financial affairs. We live in a highly charged economic environment. We can hardly listen to the radio or television for more than a few minutes without getting messages about how to earn money, save money, or spend money. The reality is that only we, with our sharpened pencil in front of the many pieces of paper that describe our financial situation, can make those decisions which will free us to live our life with abundance and harmony.

"Taking it with you isn't nearly so important

as making it last until you're ready to go."

Anonymous

Planning for the long-term can seem daunting.

Only we with our sharpened pencil,
in front of the many pieces of paper
that describe our financial situation,
can make these decisions.

Pay Yourself First?

- Your first responsibility when you get your pay check is to "pay yourself" by setting aside a special fund for retirement.

- You can do this by having an automatic withholding from your paycheck each month.

- Only when you have set aside money for the long-term do you start to pay your current bills.

- This is like paying a mortgage on your house, but instead, you are investing in your future well-being.

PAUSE FOR REFLECTION

What Does Retirement Mean to You?

How much of your future dreams depend on your control over time?

Do you know what it costs per month to live:

In a retirement home?

Assisted living?

Nursing home?

Spend a few hours checking out these facilities in your area.

Decline in the Value of a Dollar

List several regular purchases and their current costs.

If the dollar loses 50% of its value in 10 years what would your income have to be in order for you to continue to buy these daily essentials ten years from now?

Financial Analysis

Take the previous exercise further, and create a yearly budget for the present, five, and ten years into the future. Don't forget to factor in the loss of the value of a dollar.

Looking at your financial assets and comparing them with your projected costs, when will you achieve financial independence?

Spending Money Wisely

Think of a situation in which your money did not go as far as you thought it would. What corrections did you make?

Investing Wisely

Consider the current economic climate. Do you feel satisfied that you are investing your money well enough to support yourself in your later years?

Diversification of Investments

What does diversify mean to you?

How have you assured your financial future by not putting "all your eggs in one basket?"

Currently, the government pays out Social Security benefits to people over 65. At what age will you be eligible for Social Security?

It is projected that some people may not receive Social Security until they are 75 years old. If you are in that age group, how will that affect your financial plans?

What proportion of your retirement income will depend on Social Security?

We have described in detail how to be sure you are getting your money's worth. No matter how well you think you manage, it might be interesting to keep track of your expenses for one week to see where your money goes.

Keep a record of every penny you spend.

The king is like so many of us.

>*He tried to put on someone else's happiness.*

"Financial independence is not an end, but a means
to build a meaningful life."

James E. Stowers

In a recent conversation, James E. Stowers said, *"If a person has a lot of money and is not prepared to use it wisely, he may miss the fulfillment of a good and meaningful life."* We could expand this to say a person who has many resources such as experience, money, and social influence, has an opportunity to go beyond the scope of his own pleasure and help many people.

Wealth and a good position in society do not necessarily result in a meaningful life because we are constantly comparing ourselves with others. We need to search our own values to find fulfillment.

In Search for Fulfillment

Once upon a time a king was roaming through his kingdom in search of happiness. He asked his subjects of all ranks and ages, "What is the secret of happiness?" In his travels, he chanced upon a beggar sitting in the shade of a tree eating a chunk of bread and olives. He was whistling a cheery tune. The king stopped, intrigued by this poor man who, though he had nothing, seemed the most contented of men. "Why are you so happy?" he asked the beggar.

"I am happy to be alive. I have this lovely tree which provides me with shade. I have a delicious meal of bread and olives, and after my lunch, I have the reward of the gentle breeze caressing me into a deep sleep."

The king thought about this for a moment. He, too, had shade when he wanted it, more than enough to eat, a wonderful soft bed and musicians to lull him into sleep. Yet he was not happy. Finally, he asked the beggar for a favor. "Will you trade me your sack and sandals, for my warm cape and new shoes?"

"It would be an honor to serve you, my King," replied the beggar.

> *"Economic success falls short as a measure of well-being, in part because materialism can negatively influence well-being...happiness comes from social relationships, enjoyable work, fulfillment, and a sense that life has meaning."*
>
> Ed Diener, PhD and
> Martin Seligman, PhD,
> Psychologists

The king picked up the sack and put on the sandals. Handing the beggar his cloak he set off whistling along the road. But the day was hot and his feet soon got sore in the sandals. He found a tree and sat beneath it. But the shade did not comfort him. The breeze did not lull him to sleep. The king was as miserable as before.

The king is like so many of us. **He confused what he owned for a state of mind.** He tried to put on someone else's happiness. It is part of being human to look at what others have and feel that **they** have what it takes to be happy. The reality is we have to find happiness and fulfillment in ourselves. We can have a measure of happiness by engaging in activities or hobbies we have a passion for. However, to achieve long-term fulfillment, we would be wise to focus on bringing happiness to others.

Many of us plan for, talk about, and look forward to retirement as a time of fulfillment. Finally, we will have time to do all the things we put off doing for so long. Finally, we can do what we want to do when we want to do it. But will our dreams become reality?

What Does Retirement Mean?

The word retirement for most people is a one-time event, the end of working life and the beginning of a life of leisure. For others, retirement assumes a meaning that does not truly describe what actually happens. For them, it is a dreaded state which feels like being put out to pasture – a feeling that their lives as useful individuals have come to an end. There are still others for whom retirement has no meaning because life for them is a constant challenge to change and adapt their talent and experience to create a meaningful life past the arbitrary retirement age.

To me, when I retire it is not really "retire," it's a transitioning out of a full-time job into something else that I can do on my own terms. I don't want to play golf seven days a week. I want to be able to do something to continue to really live. If I make some money at it, fine; if I don't, I'm not going to worry about it too much. Bob Brush

---

Being Content With What We Have Is One Measure of Happiness.

"One can buy a house, but not a home.

One can buy a bed, but not sleep.

One can buy a clock, but not time.

One can buy a book, but not knowledge.

One can buy prestige, but not respect.

One can buy health care, but not health.

One can buy sex, but not love."

Ancient Chinese wisdom

The idea of retiring from working life is a relatively recent social invention. In 1935, as part of the New Deal, the U.S. government began sending Social Security payments to people of a certain age. This was a program initiated by Franklin D. Roosevelt to promote economic recovery during the Depression. Since then, it has been customary to set arbitrary limits on the length of our working life. Some businesses require that employees retire by age 65. In some professions, such as law, there is no age limit. In other work environments, a strict age limit is imposed in order to create employment for younger people in the trade.

However, for many of us, the late middle years, the years we may be required to retire, are precisely those years when we are at the peak of our intellectual powers.

As I work on the many projects at Stowers Innovations and other projects of my own, I have the same excitement and feeling of accomplishment I had in my earlier careers. In fact, at this time in my life I feel I have within me the ability (emotionally, intellectually, and physically) to explore and give new meaning to my life and the lives of those around me. I start each day with a hope that I can continue to create new ideas and inspire others to be the best they can be. This is what gives my life meaning. It is the way I am still actively engaged in the world around me.   Jack

After many years in a career, most of us will have accumulated experiences and skills which make us more valuable to society than ever before. Our termination from useful employment at age 65 may spell a premature end to the opportunity to share our gifts. This forced retirement is as much a loss to society as it is to those forced to retire. However, **if we become financially independent**, we gain security, freedom of action and choices without the constraints of earning a living.

*Retirement ...
it is a dreaded state
which feels like being
put out to pasture.*

We have more choices about how we will share our talents and hard-earned skills with others.

Let's substitute for the word retirement the word **change** – a change in the way we use our time. In his nineties, Picasso continued to create new styles and experimented with new media until he could no longer hold a brush in his hand. He said, ***"It takes a long time to grow young."***

When we retire, at whatever age, we are going to choose a new direction in our life. We will be standing at a crossroads. The possibilities may seem limitless. Are we going to choose something meaningful, satisfying, and compelling?

Many women have had the opportunity to try a variety of vocations as they cycle in and out of the work force. Rose Stolowy, who just turned 92, was a pioneer in changing career directions. Here is her story.

"It takes a long time

to grow young."

I've had a lot of jobs, and they were all good. Out of school, I got a job at the Columbia National Bank and worked there for two years. But, then, of course, I got married right away. And then I spent time at home being a hausfrau and a mother. When my youngest was seven and my oldest was 14, the doctor advised me to get a job because the children were in school and I did not have enough activity at home.

I had no real work skills, so I thought, "Why don't I go into business?" It was an exciting idea. I said to my precious husband, "You know what, if you give me $1,000, I'll see what I can do with it." In 1944, that was a lot of money. I was always sewing and doing embroidery and needlepoint, so I went into the fabric business. I handled the uniform fabrics for the Catholic schools and designed the uniforms. I had the business for 14 years.

Then my mother got sick and needed me. My father had passed away and she was a typical hausfrau. She couldn't do it alone in her house so she came to live with us. So I began to volunteer at Menorah Hospital and I continued to do that for more than 20 years.

Then my husband sold his business, but he just couldn't retire. He said, "Honey, that's not for me." So he started a new business, S & R Tailors, and I went in with him as his bookkeeper and accountant...a brand new venture for me. But I got my name on the business...R for Rose and S for Sol. I learned how to do accounting and I made out the payroll and taxes. I still do my own taxes. We had that business for ten years before we sold it.

Rose Stolowy had many occasions to ask herself, "What does life have for me now? Which path shall I take?"

If we look at retirement with this attitude, it will take on a totally different meaning: not the end of life as we know it, but the beginning of a new adventure. Retirement acquires a new meaning if we disregard its association with retire from the world. Instead, we can cultivate our imagination, take up the challenge of using our new found opportunities of time, and find more meaning in life.

"La Fortuna favorisce gli audaci"

"Dame Fortune favors those who dare" says this old Italian saying. Human beings are endowed with a nature that is an open and constantly evolving system. Some of us welcome changes provided we do not face too many of them at once. If we are determined to make the best use of our precious gift of time, change can be an adventure, not a trauma. But do we have the courage and determination to embrace our opportunities?

When we are faced with the challenges of leaving the 8 to 5 world of work, it helps to systematically explore opportunities one at a time. Here are five steps you can use to help you plan creatively for change.

1. **Self-evaluation:** What strengths do you have which will help you cope with changes? Of what value are your intellectual assets, experience, talents, and passion? What have you dreamed of doing that you have not yet had time to do?

Second Acts

"No matter what your age or stage in life, you can lead the life you have always wanted and create a more rewarding future."

Stephen Pollan, who wrote these words, believes that,

"The main reason for career is money, the fuel for quality of life. But for fulfillment, we often must look elsewhere."

He believes that we can have a Second Act any time we are willing to accept the possibility of a new life.

Stephen Pollan
Author

2. **Research.** You can expand your horizon by looking at what options are available. You can get the facts you need by visiting or connecting with people who share your interests.

3. **Test.** Experience in a small way an activity you might like to pursue. For example, plan a trip to the country in which you would like to live to check out cost of living, health care and ease of becoming part of the community.

4. **Evaluate.** Look at your financial resources, time constraints and life priorities and weigh them against a trial run.

5. **Decide.**

- Can you make this change and keep your family relationships intact?

  - Does your health support the pursuit of this opportunity?

    - Can you pursue this activity and not deplete your financial resources?

    - Is there a good fit between your financial resources and hopes for the future?

    - Does your passion and determination warrant spending your time and money?

What have you dreamed of doing that you have not yet had time to do?

Self-esteem and Identity

We may be subject to an identity crisis at retirement if we have focused only on our career. At work, we have a defined role, a social network, a feeling of being part of a team, a sense of competence, structure, and financial security. All these important factors contribute to our self-esteem and identity. Their loss may result in depression.

Because it is only recently that people have lived long after retirement age, most of us have not thought of what we will do. When we lose the continuity our career environment had given us, are we ready for a new phase in our life?

One woman described the sense of aimlessness of her father-in-law after he retired from an active and successful business career. Although he did some work in the community, she recalled:

> *I can still remember his wife being beside herself because he was at her side all the time. He wanted to go to the grocery store with her, he wanted to be with her in the kitchen. I mean, this was a woman who had had a husband off to work 7 to 7 Monday through Friday, and all of a sudden he's there! This was a very bright man, who had had a wonderful job!*
>
> Karen

Is it possible to foresee and prepare for the life that comes after retirement? Karen's father-in-law had dreamed of a leisurely life enlivened by daily golf games at his club. He was unprepared for the reality that daily games of golf were not enough to sustain his feelings of self-worth.

On the other hand, Renata Stanton, a travel agent who worked until she was 77, has been delighted the last two years to simply enjoy a life of leisure. *"As hard as I have worked all my life, I am delighted to be able to live life more slowly. To savor the little things in life."*

However, those who plan to leave a lifelong career in their mid to late 60's may be shocked to find their dreams of retirement do not pan out. How can we continue to use our competence and interpersonal skills to make our later years meaningful? Do we have hobbies or interests that bring passion to our life? In short, beyond our career, where can we find satisfaction? It is important to plan a gradual transition from one stage in life to the next.

We can be contented if we live within our means, have an appreciation for life, and are engaged in activities that bring us joy. However, our life will have more meaning, and our happiness will be sustainable if we can reach out to help others.

They Won't Go

Discussing the tricky issue of dealing with aging executives who don't want to retire, Professor Bennis (age 78) asked how we know when someone is over the hill? *"How do you create a social system where you can maintain the self-esteem of the person who is being asked to leave?"* Many highly successful and well paid people measure their self-worth by where they work, so they have to be pushed, unless they are too big and powerful to oust.

Patrick McGeehan, Reporter
The New York Times

Creating a Meaningful Life

In her poem, *"When Death Comes,"* Mary Oliver deals with the issue of looking back and wondering if we really value the life we have lived. Here is an excerpt.

Happiness will be sustainable if we can reach out to help others.

When it is over, I want to say: All my life

I was a bride married to amazement.

I was the bridegroom, taking the world into my arms.

When it's over, I don't want to wonder

If I have made of my life something particular, and real.

I don't want to find myself sighing and frightened,

Or full of argument.

I don't want to end up simply having visited this world.

We do not set out to make of our lives *"something particular and real"* anymore than we find happiness by setting out to be wealthy. We become financially independent by consistent and determined saving and investing. We make our life meaningful as we work tirelessly to develop our talents and skills, and share them with others.

When we have a passion for doing something, we never tire of improving our skill. A great photographer never tires of trying to get the perfect photograph. A good pianist never tires of getting a piece "just right." At first, all of our focus is on learning our skill. Finally, the day comes when we are proficient and confident enough to want to share what we have achieved with others. We may do this by teaching the skills we have developed or by sharing our creative vision in a performance, an exhibition, or a publication.

The relay racer does not dwell on getting to the end of the race. He is intent only on running at top form, his particular lap. In the relay race of life, we do not know how many laps we will be able to run. To feel satisfied with our "race" we concentrate on running each lap as well and as joyfully as we can. Each lap may emphasize different aspects of our lives. But with confidence and self-esteem, our vision of our place in the world becomes more clear. Finally, in the closing laps of the race, our talents and commitment to helping others can come to full flower.

It is possible that many of us will have 30 or more years of active living past the age of 65. With a lifetime of experience and resources, these later years could turn out to be the most meaningful ones, in which sharing takes on a whole new dimension.

One knows from daily life that one exists for other people. First of all, for those upon whose smiles and well-being our own happiness is wholly dependent, and then for the many, unknown to us, to whose destinies we are bound by the ties of sympathy. A hundred times every day I remind myself that my inner and outer life are based on the labors of other men, living and dead, and that I must exert myself in order to give in the same measure as I have received and am still receiving.

Albert Einstein

A Meaningful Life

A World Values Survey conducted between 1981 and 2001 found that 58% of Americans say that they often think about the meaning and purpose of life.

...in the closing laps of the race, our talents and commitment to helping others can come to flower.

PAUSE FOR REFLECTION

The Meaning in Your Life

What brings meaning to your life at this time?

Can you foresee a time when that which gives your life meaning may change?

Fortune Favors Those Who Dare

Think of a major life change you will face.

Try the creative Planning for Change strategy on page 66 to help with your plans.

Self-Worth and Identity

What makes a significant contribution to your feelings of self-worth?

On what is your identity based?

Describe who you were 10 years ago. Compare that list with who you are today.

In Search of Happiness

What brings you happiness today?

Did this happiness come from an inner source, or from a comparison with others?

"For a variety of reasons, they (many retirees) are not able to recover from their pre-retirement failure to hone old skills, develop new ones or make and nurture necessary personal contacts. As a result, they fail in their first attempts to realize their retirement dreams...and many simply settle into the recliner and turn on the TV."

Ralph Warner
Author

The Best Things in Life Are Free

List some of the best, free things in your life.

The Bride Married to Amazement

How have you made of your life "something particular and real?"

To what do you passionately devote your time?

Sharing with Others

What are the special talents and interests that you can share to make a difference in the lives and well-being of others?

Giving It All Away

Chester Carlson, the inventor of the Xerox machine, worked tirelessly to perfect his invention. After 20 years of trying to find backers, and trying to get his machine to work reliably, he was successful.

Now, he had money to spare. Instead of treating himself to things he had done without, he spent the rest of his life giving his fortune away in an attempt to realize his ambition of "dying a poor man."

David Owen
Biographer

SOCIAL WELL-BEING

4

I am so glad you are here.

"I am so glad you are here... It helps me realize

how beautiful my world is."

Rainer Maria Rilke

These words of Rilke are a perfect definition of social well-being; for even though we may need time alone every now and then, we cannot exist alone for long. Our well-being is dependent on the warm, welcoming presence of others. Our ability to reach our potential requires the support and input of other people.

Most of us rely on family, close friends, or neighbors for comfort and support. For others, professional and social organizations are a primary source of support. These relationships give us a feeling of belonging and security.

Although we are born into a social environment, we need to build and maintain the social network that gives us a feeling of well-being in our adult years. These days, social scientists use the term social capital to describe the social resources we develop over time.

Unlike financial capital, social capital cannot be inherited unless we live in a small town all our lives. Even in a small town, though, the people who experience the most social well-being have developed social skills that they can draw on to sustain them throughout their lives.

To develop the social capital that will sustain us all our whole life, we need to:

- Foster and maintain meaningful friendships.

- Learn the skills necessary to have relationships that last over time.

- Learn the social graces we need to help us navigate smoothly in the environment in which we live.

People need people, and people with good social skills draw others to them so they can support and be supported, love and be loved, cherish and be cherished. Our relationships have many levels of commitment. Social capital is the resource which helps us connect to all of society with its many formal and informal relationships.

Social Capital

Social capital can be simply described as a person's social skills: popularity, list of contacts, facility in dealing with others, and charisma. A person's stock of social capital can be measured by the number of organizations to which he belongs. If a person invests in social capital when young, he reaps the benefits when he is older. The more one invests, the more one has to gain.

Edward Glaeser, PhD and
David Laibson, PhD
Economists

FRIENDSHIP: *The Cornerstone of Social Well-Being*

*The fabric of our lives
is colored and strengthened
by our diverse friendships.*

"Wishing to be friends is quick work, but friendship

is a slow ripening fruit."

Aristotle

What is a Friend?

Who can we call in the middle of the night when we have a crisis? Who drives us to the hospital if we are suddenly taken ill? When we think of our happiest moments in life, who comes immediately to mind?

We share our interests and enjoy the adventure of pursuing them with our friends. With our closest friends, the people who know us best, we may feel safe in sharing our heartfelt secret desires and personal failures. The fabric of our lives is colored and strengthened by our diverse friendships. In 1935, acknowledging the importance of friendship in our lives, the United States Congress proclaimed the first Sunday in August as National Friendship Day.

Friendships are the relationships we spend the most time cultivating. Not all of our friends are equally integrated into our lives. Friendships develop for different reasons and settle into various levels of commitment which we can describe as *friends for a reason, friends for a season, and friends for life.*

Friends for a Reason

Friendships that form for a reason are often short-lived because we usually are not sharing many aspects of our lives with these friends. For example, we may begin a friendship with someone we meet at our local tennis club or neighborhood court. If our contact with this person is focused on tennis games, we will know little about him beyond what a terrific backhand he has. We may enjoy playing tennis with this person, but it is possible to replace him with someone equally skilled.

These days we might meet someone who shares our special interest in an internet chat room. For example, searching for quilting patterns, we might get an e-mail response from someone who has the pattern we are looking for. Soon an e-mail

> *"The proper office of a friend is to side with us when we are in the wrong. Nearly anybody will side with you when you are in the right."*
>
> Mark Twain

relationship begins. This friendship could be short-lived, ending when we have what we were looking for. However, it could develop into a long-term relationship which branches out beyond our shared interest.

Friendships for a reason may form during times of stress or transition. One person we interviewed described a friend as her "hard transition friend." Their reason for being together is to help each other through transitions. However, they have different perspectives on life in general, and when things are going well with them individually, the friendship does not endure. Both women seem comfortable that they are friends for a reason and it is okay not to be together when the crisis has passed.

Another example of a friendship that begins for a reason is a mentoring relationship. It starts with a desire on the part of one person who has a skill to teach and another who seeks to learn that skill. As the two work together, a lifelong

friendship could blossom. But the original intent is the desire of two people to share: a grateful giver and a grateful receiver. When the reason for the mentoring no longer exists, the relationship may end. We may have nothing in common with this friend beyond our need for computer help and computer skills.

However, as with other friends for a reason, we may find that our friendship with a mentor evolves into a deeper commitment that may last for many years. It is when people share many life experiences that they are bonded by their support of each other.

Friendships that form for a reason are often short-lived because we usually are not sharing many aspects of our lives with these friends.

Friends for a Season

If we think of our life experience as seasons, we might better understand the times we have drifted apart from people who once were our friends. This can be a wrenching experience the first time it happens.

Little children are so excited when they come home from school and, for the first time, declare that a certain person is their friend. They are discerning about who is their friend, though they may be sensitive enough not to disparage other children. One little person says simply, "He is not my favorite," when she talks of those she is not close to.

Sometimes these first friendships are very fleeting, with the children declaring that they are friends forever one minute and going home in a huff the next. However, as children get older and more capable of commitment, these early friendships can be very intense. To a third grader, for example, it can seem like a tragedy when she finds in September that her "best" friend is not in the same classroom.

These childhood friendships can be torn apart because parents move; or worse, the "best" friend develops different interests or friends. Early on, children must learn gracefully to accept that some friendships are not lifelong.

As adults, we have many friends for a season. Perhaps we are very close to a neighbor when our children are in the same school. Or a special person next door becomes a friend but does not stay connected to us when she moves away.

Many of us form friendships at work that relate only to work. It does not seem likely that these friendships will carry over into our personal lives after we part ways.

A man who has worked for the same company all his adult life has begun to wonder how many of his work friends will be part of his post retirement network.

Sometimes these first friendships are very fleeting.

Quite frankly, I'm jealous of all the friendship networking my wife has now. Women do a better job of communicating than men do. You don't realize that until you start saying, "Well, what am I going to do after I retire?"   Bob Brush

These friendships for a season are based on location, interests, or a time of life, and do not stand the test of time because we do not invest enough of ourselves in these relationships. We need to learn to be grateful for what they offered us and gracefully move on when the relationship can no longer be sustained.

Friends for Life

True friendship has no time, distance, or age limit. People of different generations can be friends for life. People of different races or cultures have been known to form deep, long-lasting friendships.

These friends for life relationships are so deep that they may survive long absences or lack of contact. For many of us, these relationships begin at school, sometimes as early as grade school. However, most lifelong friendships begin between ages 15 and 25, according to research by Hallmark Cards. For many adults, a "best friend" is like a family member. Here is a typical example:

"Where have you been all my life?"

I am still friends with some of the people I knew in high school. In many respects, my friends are my family. We've gone through a lot together. We may not see each other for five or ten years and we meet and we pick up from yesterday as if no time has past. That is just great!

Peggy Wrightsman

It is often the case that a friendship starts without our knowing it; maybe it was something in the way that person shook our hand, or walked, or laughed. We ask, "Where have you been all my life?" We get an unexplained feeling that we would like to know each other more. We are compelled to talk, and then find we really connect. Respect follows and soon we find more and more reasons to share experiences.

When we are with a close friend, we feel good; we laugh easily. The friendship began because the two people were open to each other and the relationship continued to deepen as their involvement grew. Friends for life often have supported each other through many major life events.

I did not meet my closest friend until we were in our late twenties. We were both new mothers, new to the neighborhood. For over 30 years we have supported each other through struggles like miscarriages, divorce, chronic illness, and death. We have celebrated graduations, marriages, new careers, and grandchildren. She is a sister to me, my friend for life. Even when we are in different countries she is on my mind and in my heart.
                                                                    Anonymous

It is common for people in a very close friendship to share a stronger bond than they do with a sibling or other family member. Even people in strong happy marriages may feel closer to their friends than to their spouses, unless their best friend is their spouse.

Marriage: Friendship and Partnership

In some cultures, marriage is an economic or political contract between two families who want an alliance. Sometimes, children are promised to each other while they are still in their mother's womb. In these cultures, where the marriage is primarily a partnership, the emotional ties may be found outside the family.

Today, in Western cultures, it is generally assumed that it is love and friendship which draws people into marriage. Passionate love alone does not necessarily result in a lasting marriage. A marriage between friends starts with shared interests; and even when there are setbacks, the couple works to overcome them.

> *"We cannot tell the precise moment when friendship is formed. As in filling a vessel drop by drop, there is at last a drop which makes it run over; so in a series of kindnesses there is at last one which makes the heart run over."*
>
> Samuel Johnson

We've had our ups and downs, but we really work at it. In our kitchen we have our family motto, "Learn from yesterday, Plan for tomorrow, and Challenge today." Some people get into the habit of bad things being comfortable for them. We don't want to do that. We want to move on and get better.　　　Glenda Spellerberg

Glenda and her husband have shared a variety of experiences, supporting each others' needs and enjoying a long, comfortable relationship.

We play many roles throughout our marriages: at one time or another, we may be friends, lovers, parents, and partners. Each couple has strengths, and each role is prominent at different times in the marriage. A couple married for more than 30 years faced serious difficulties when one of their parents was ill, and another was having trouble with finances. They were delighted to find how well they worked together and supported each other during stressful times.

As we have matured and grown older we have been strong in different areas at different times. But in these past months, I can't help but reflect on how well we have worked together. My God, what a great team we have become!　　　Karen Brush

Two people, sharing experiences, supporting each others' needs, enjoying each other and working toward a common goal, can cultivate a friendship that gives their marriage a chance to endure.

> *"Nothing opens the heart like a true friend to whom you may impart griefs, joys, fears, hopes...and whatever lies upon the heart."*
>
> Francis Bacon

Making It Through the Night

I lay by your side as you breathed in and out.

You talked in your sleep and you tossed all about.

Of what were you dreaming, was it friends we have known?

Or was it the children before they were grown?

But I lay there thinking and worrying, too.

If you rode on ahead, just what would I do?

If I were the one to be left all alone,

How would I manage to be on my own?

Our 60-year marriage has had a long run.

I now know the meaning of "two become one."

I start a sentence, you finish it for me.

I lose my way, you still can see.

But enough of that thinking, why dwell on sorrow?

I must be happy while we still have tomorrow.

Mary Grant

> *"Loving ourselves and others, and being very present with that connection, is what makes us happy, at any age."*
>
> Kathleen Caldwell

Our Animal Friends

Some people live with minimum contact with others because of age or physical disability. For them, friendships become even more valuable and important to their need for belonging. Without a friend to care for and to care about us, it is not easy to accept the sometimes difficult realities of life. Many people who live alone get their feeling of connection by having an animal friend. They love and care for their pet, and in return it becomes a source of comfort and love. People who live alone are generally happier and healthier if they own a pet, and find it easier to accept life as it comes.

Companions

We are out for a walk in the forest,
Dog and me.
I obediently walk the path.
She, preferring the untrod way,
Bounds through the underbrush.
This companionship of ours
Is a loosely constructed thing.
Dog bounds off, out of sight
Eagerly pursuing the unseen in the forest's depth.
I scuff the leaves along the path,
Alone, yet, accompanied.

Leaving the forest I climb a hill,
A mountain in a sea of prairie.
Resting against a warm stone
I find dog's eyes begging.

Many people who live alone get their feeling of connection by having an animal friend.

I rub her ears.
She wags her tail.
The wind caresses my cheek.

Standing, we eye the open field.
Dog looks at me with anticipation
And we are off!
Racing down the hill,
Tumbling over ourselves with joy,
For life!
For movement!
For companionship!

Then, dog runs off again.
I walk on alone,
Accompanied.

Back at my cottage, dog is there
Wagging the porch off.
Sitting on the step together
Her head on my lap,
We are one.

S.G. Hope

Dog is there...we are one.

Friendship is Like a Garden

Traveling around the country and abroad, we are in awe when we see a vision of beauty and the irrepressible life and growth all around us. Through the cracks in the rocks, there emerges a clump of beautiful daisies. We might see a cultivated garden that adds color and beauty to the house and surroundings.

Flowers, just like friendships, reward us with splendor and enjoyment year after year when we cultivate them with care and attention. But just like flowers, friendships wither and die through neglect and lack of nourishment. The irrepressible wildflower that blooms in the most unlikely places can be likened to those expressions of friendship that surprise us and come from people whom we have not "cultivated." They appear in our lives for a brief moment and make a lasting impression.

More often, however, friends find time for each other. This can be as formal as the meeting of a book club or a school reunion; or it could be getting together for a cup of coffee or a walk around the neighborhood. We need to share our life story, and to talk about our troubles and joys. We need to be held when we are sad, listened to when we are troubled, and danced with when we are full of joy. This is what a friendship is for. This is how our lives are enriched and made more meaningful.

We may start a relationship with a spontaneous burst of enthusiasm, but real friendship is built up slowly and stands the test of time. The first bright spark needs to be fed slowly by empathy, acceptance, and trust. Finally, a warm fire, with a bank of slow burning embers, is created, fed by the winds of understanding. Each of us brings something to the fire of our relationship. If one person's energy to maintain the fire fades, the fire threatens to go out. Without reciprocity it can be too much for one person to keep a relationship going.

Friendship is the model for all relationships. However, from friends for a reason to the deeper intimacy of a good marriage, all meaningful relationships share common characteristics: commitment, respect, empathy, acceptance, trust, and humor.

Varieties of Flowers in Your Friendship Garden

Just as our garden has many kinds of flowers, so we have many kinds of friends. Here are few varieties of friends:

The best friend

The old friend

The mentor

The new friend

The ex-friend

The boss friend

The airplane friend

The confidant

The e-mail friend

The special interest friend

The friend's friend

PAUSE FOR REFLECTION

What is a Friend?

What do you think are the essentials of friendship?

When you hear the word "friend" who comes to mind?

Who would be there for you in an emergency?

Friends for a Reason

Think of someone who has been your *friend for a reason*.

Have you had a *friend for a reason* who became a *friend for life*?

Friends for a Season

Who have been your *friends for a season*?

How have you tried to keep in contact with those friends?

Friends for Life

How did you meet your *friend for life*?

What qualities set your *friend for life* apart from other friends?

How do you keep your friendship alive?

Marriage: Friendship and Partnership

Were your grandparents friends as well as partners?

How would you characterize your parents' marriage?

What changes have you seen in marriage during your lifetime?

Our Animal Friends

Think about your first animal friend.

What did it bring to your life?

We may start a friendship with a spontaneous burst of enthusiasm.

There is not a substitute for close friends
who will be there for us through thick and thin.

"To be able to find joy in another's joy,

that is the secret of happiness."

George Bernanos

Our lives become more meaningful when we do things with and for others, creating the kinds of connections that will enable us to live our lives fully. Positive, spontaneous relationships are possible, but building a social fabric that will sustain us usually takes time and care. Two new trends provide opportunities for us to make connections with others: the "Third Place" and the virtual village of the internet.

Are Virtual Relationships Real?

People are rediscovering the need for a place to hang out away from work and home that is not a traditional bar. These "Third Places" are relaxed and welcoming settings which are like an oasis away from the responsibilities of life. A place where we can come to talk, share stories, and make new friends. "Third Places" have the same function as the town square in a small town. People need people after all.

Such a place, however, is not a substitute for close friends who will be there for us through thick and thin.

The Internet is another place where people go in order to feel connected. Many have personal web sites and "blogs" in which they pour out their personal stories to strangers. People respond to those in trouble with money and regular e-mails of encouragement. Some, who may be hesitant to be intimately involved with their neighbor, are emboldened by the anonymity of the internet to create a virtual intimacy with strangers.

Like the relationships of the "Third Place," internet relationships give a person a feeling of being in control. There is a lot of emotional freedom in these types of relationships.

Third Places

"Third places remain upbeat because those who enjoy them ration the time they spend there. They leave when or before the magic begins to fade."

Ray Oldenburg, PhD
Sociologist

Are these virtual relationships real? Yes, however, they are only a small part of what a person needs for social well-being. A critical quality missing in these relationships is the type of commitment that comes from physical presence. These spontaneous, anonymous relationships can fill a void, but building a social fabric that will sustain us takes commitment, time, and care.

Commitment to Maintaining Relationships

A commitment is the mortar that holds people together. It is an unwritten contract we live up to in order to feel connected. It is an understanding we have which binds us emotionally and intellectually to another person or to our work. We learn that when we give of ourselves through our time and talent, we, in return, receive what we need to thrive. This interdependence will shape our lives.

For most of us, the path to understanding the value of commitment begins very early with the tender loving care we get in our families. Later, we learn the art of getting along with others by interacting with our siblings, cousins, and classmates. With our playmates we practice maintaining the kind of connections that make friendships binding.

As we seek to satisfy our aspirations, we realize that each of us has dreams we want to fulfill. Our commitment to our work, to those who support us, and those who need us, builds our social capital. In the end, we discover strengths we did not know we had.

One of the keys to good relationships is a commitment to assuming a responsibility for maintaining them. When he was a medical student, Jim Stowers realized that he needed to help people, but not as a doctor.

After my Air Force experience and years of medical training I dreamed of becoming financially independent. I never dwelt on profits, but rather on how I could help people who trusted me with their earnings, to become successful over time. I never expected the extraordinary success I have achieved.

"It is one of the most beautiful compensations of life that no man can sincerely try to help another without helping himself."

Ralph Waldo Emerson

Along with an intense desire to help other people be successful, Jim applied an unwavering determination, integrity, and years of hard work to accomplish his goal. Now, along with making others successful, his own success has enabled him to help others in another way, through the endowment he and his wife set up for the Stowers Institute for Medical Research.

Each of us has an opportunity to commit ourselves to helping others. We may give money to our favorite cause, work for an organization whose values we support, or help individuals who need our time and efforts. Sometimes, our commitment to others may take the form of doing small favors for our neighbors.

We live very busy lives with work, family, personal health, friendships, and reaching out to strangers. We must consciously balance our priorities as they shift throughout our lives. When she feels overwhelmed by all her obligations, Tina Sprinkle says to herself, *"Wait a minute, what is more important: getting this project done, or spending quality time with my friend or family?"*

Following through with our commitments to relationships, work, and self, helps us build an integrity which inspires respect and trust in people around us.

Respect

As a measure of one's respect for others, all traditions and cultures rely on some version of the Golden Rule: *Treat others as* **you** *would like to be treated.* If we change the focus from ourselves to others by rephrasing the rule, *"Treat others as* **they** *would like to be treated,"* we will achieve the full measure of what respect means. When we receive this kind of expression of respect, we feel valued for what we are, not for what others want us to be.

Jim Stowers applied an unwavering determination, integrity, and years of hard work to accomplish his goal.

When we practice the rule of treating others as they would like to be treated, we can derive an immense satisfaction as we watch them grow in self-esteem. They begin to live up to their dream of who they want to be.

Sheelagh's granddaughter, who was only 4, wanted to carry a full bowl of soup to the table. Her mother stood back and quietly watched, albeit with bated breath, as a confident child carefully and successfully put the soup on the table. ***"I did it!"*** *she declared, smiling with pride. This mother had allowed the child to try to be like a grown up. The child had succeeded and gained in self-esteem.*

Treat others as they would like to be treated.

What passes for respect will vary from culture to culture. For example, in the 60s in Japan, older widows of retirement age could be seen with large shears, sitting on the grassy slopes in a park cutting the grass. This seemed very inefficient and unimportant, but it was really a wonderful idea. The women felt useful and earned a little money; the grass was beautifully cut; and the environment was not polluted by noisy lawn mowers. The older women in this culture felt some dignity and self-respect in having a role to play in beautifying their city.

Since the amendment giving women the equal right to vote, there has been a gradual shift in the courtesies which once created a sense of civility between men and women. The following examples are behaviors that are no longer expected:

- Holding the door open.
- Tipping your hat.
- Walking on the outside of the sidewalk.
- Giving up your seat on a bus.
- Paying for a meal at a restaurant.

Today, some people find the blurring of distinctions between the sexes confusing. They may disregard social graces because of the uncertainty in knowing what is acceptable. This may cause some misunderstanding, or at least, a sense that the world has grown less civil. However, what was once a prescription for the behavior of men towards women is now mutual respect, where people, regardless of age or sex, are aware of treating others with courtesy.

Our social fabric is woven with the threads of respect for each other. If we impose change on others, they will lose their sense of dignity and self-worth.

Empathy and Sympathy: Reaching Out With Understanding

We are born with a capacity for empathy because we all need others' kindness. We may think of empathy as a spontaneous feeling, but the Dalai Lama allies empathy with reason and regards it as a trait that we can develop. *When we direct our mental faculties onto our feelings of empathy, we find that not only can we enhance them, we can transform them into love and compassion itself.* We can cultivate our sensitivity to others by paying attention to how we feel when we are in someone else's presence. Then we can use our powers of reasoning to decide what action needs to be taken and how much help we can give in a committed way.

Just as we can develop our sensitivity and capacity for empathy, we can also desensitize ourselves to empathy. There is a controversy today about the influence of violence on television and in pop music. Some psychologists feel that an overexposure to this virtual violence desensitizes a child to tragedy and could, therefore, diminish their capacity for empathy.

Walk a mile in their shoes.

Cultivating Empathy

Children in good preschools learn a lot about empathy. For example, when they are learning to share toys, children are taught to think how they would feel if no one shared with them. Or if a child is aggressive to another child, the teacher may ask the child to remember how it feels to be hit.

Many preschools begin the day with "Circle Time" during which children share stories about their lives and bring things in to share. During this time, children are learning to support each other during sad times and also to share others' happiness. This is the beginning of practicing empathy.

Although we usually associate empathy with feeling another's pain, we are empathic to all the feelings of others: tiredness, joy, anger, fear, happiness. This is also true for sympathy. People sometimes confuse sympathy with empathy. In the Italian language, when we describe someone we may say "molto simpatico," which means that we have a spontaneous good feeling about that man, and we feel happy to be in his presence.

In our country, we usually think of sympathy in terms of understanding someone else's sadness. We express sympathy and send sympathy cards to someone who has lost a loved one, is fired from a job, or has had an accident. We may not "feel" their pain but we imagine how we would feel in that situation and express our concern.

When we are truly empathic, our feelings and reason will lead us to take some action to relieve the suffering of the person we feel compassion for. When we reach out to help others, we do so without expecting anything in return. Both empathy and sympathy bond us into a community of loving friends and neighbors, which give us a sense of well-being.

The network of electronic communications has given birth to "e-truism," which is another way to express our empathy for others. When we are moved to send money, pray for a stranger in trouble, or send a message of encouragement, we feel we have met our obligation to help. However, often physical presence is also required to really give people the help they need.

Some psychologists feel that an overexposure to this virtual violence desensitizes a child to tragedy...

In relationships with family and friends, our actions may require a long-term commitment. We often do not have the advantage of a community of people who can help by being present when someone is in trouble. Then, every day, we need to balance our own needs with the needs of those we love. This is one of the dilemmas of our time.

Empathy: A Path to Peace

We live in a global society with a diversity of religion, ethnicity, and lifestyle. How open we are to different points of view will determine our degree of empathy. We tend to seek out people who are like us and put up walls to distance ourselves from those who are different from us. **It takes a lot of energy to maintain a wall.**

In order to promote understanding across nations, President Eisenhower started a program in 1950 to help people exchange ideas and experiences. A number of programs are now in place for adults and children involving arts, pen pals, sports, and cultural exchange programs. These are supported by volunteers in People to People International (PTPI) chapters around the world. PTPI believes that when we understand each other we discover universal values and aspirations which lead to more tolerance of others and acceptance of differences.

We all have the same needs: love, security, opportunity, and self-respect. When we communicate with others, we can see beyond the labels of nationality, religion, or ethnicity to the person who is like us. We think the wall will make us secure; but what will lead us toward security is understanding, respect, and empathy.

What we do not know often creates fear in us. When we experience fear, our focus is self-directed for survival and we become more selfish. The challenge to practice empathy begins when we can replace fear with understanding. It is hard to fear someone when we feel what they feel, when we experience even in a small way what they experience. In this way, empathy becomes part of our daily life.

People to People International

"I have long believed, as have many before me, that peaceful relations between nations requires understanding and mutual respect between individuals."

President Dwight D. Eisenhower
Founder of People to People
International

Frankly, I was afraid at first because I was alone and it was dusk. He came at me so quickly, and he looked frightening because he was wearing a black leather jacket and his hair was spiky and a weird color. I stepped back, and he stopped. I looked into his face and saw that he was scared too, and concerned about something. His car had broken down and he was in a neighborhood where people were afraid of him. When I saw his anxiety, I calmed down. I knew what it was like to have my car break down. I offered to help

S.G.Hope

It takes a lot of energy to maintain a wall.

This woman was able to overcome her fear long enough to be empathic with a person who looked so different. Then she was able to see him as a person in distress and help him out.

As we learn to pair our empathy and sympathy with reason, we become more compassionate, less fearful, and at peace in our world.

Acceptance

Acceptance means to "receive with gladness." To this definition we can add being grateful for what we have and who we are. When we are grateful, we are more readily inclined to understand and accept different situations and points of view.

In the United States, with its variety of cultures and lifestyles, it is important to try to understand the views of others. We go beyond tolerance of different lifestyles to acceptance if we make an effort to mix and mingle. Many cities host ethnic fairs throughout the year. During these festivals people are welcome to sample food, music, dancing, and art from many countries. We broaden our own world view through these opportunities, while still cherishing our own traditions.

Perhaps the most subtle form of intolerance is the way we treat our very young and very old. Many people talk in a condescending way to children, who feel the difference and are very quick to disregard or dislike adults who "talk down" to them. Children who express their dislike for this treatment may be admonished to be polite. This is a double standard which does not model for children what respectful behavior is.

Paradoxically, as a society of youth worshippers, we often do not give older people their due. It is unfortunate to see them ignored or patronized. Hopefully, this will change as the baby boomers reach a mature age. This shift in attitude is reflected in the story below.

I have friends of all ages. It is important to me because older people have so much experience and such a broad base. They are very generous and gracious and they LISTEN. The more I know myself, the more open I am to listening. People who don't listen and think they have all the answers probably have a lot of growing up to do. More and more I am very humbled by this process.   Tina

Listening helps us understand, reach out, and accept others. Our capacity for empathy relies on our awareness of the different conditions and needs of those around us. Acceptance begins with understanding and being alert to how we can act on our empathy without hurting the self-respect and feelings of the person we want to help.

In the small environment of a neighborhood or apartment complex, we don't need to look far to find many opportunities to practice understanding, empathy, and acceptance. Find out who needs a pot of stew, who needs a ride to the grocery store, or who can be relied on for a ride to the doctor. These neighborhood connections, formed through our empathy and acceptance, are more important to our security than the presence of police or locks on our doors.

Phases of Empathy

I feel your pain:

- I want to help.

- Do I understand your needs?

- Please tell me what you need.

- Can I satisfy your need?

- I do satisfy your need.

  or

- Sorry, I cannot help you.

Giacomo Spero

Trust: Your Most Important Asset

"Treasure the trust people have in you as your most important asset. It was not given to you. You earned it over time. Once lost, it is lost forever."

James E. Stowers

When we have trust in ourselves, and we are able to trust others, we will be seen as having a good character.

Trust is a complex emotional attitude that results when we feel secure, hopeful, and optimistic that others will treat us kindly. When we trust ourselves to be kind and to fulfill our promises to others, we are more likely to be trusting of others and more able to make social connections. When we have trust in ourselves, and we are able to trust others, we will be seen as having a good character. People will see us as a person of integrity who can be depended on.

How trusting we are depends on our culture and environment. For example, in a neighborhood where people know each other, it is easier to feel secure that others will deal with us fairly.

When I was a boy, my father owned a neighborhood grocery store. People would phone my father and order their groceries. I would deliver these to their door. At the end of the month, people would come to the store with a blank, signed check and ask my father what they owed. He would look up his records and fill in the amount.

Sheldon Stahl

This comforting story illustrates the kind of trust that is possible even today in smaller communities.

Like the money we put in a bank and build up slowly to develop our financial assets, trust takes a long time to build. It is the cornerstone of good relationships. When we trust people, we are secure in the thought that they will not fail us.

How can we show that we can be trusted? Just as a bank can destroy our confidence through mismanagement, so too, we can lose the trust of a friend because of a thoughtless act. It is only through consistent behavior over time that we gain the confidence of others. It might begin with signs of sincerity at a first meeting. With good eye contact, a firm handshake, and a sincere smile, we prove that we can be relied upon; that we can be counted on to keep a promise. A fabric of mutual trust in which there are no broken threads is woven slowly over time through many small acts of kindness, commitment, and competence.

We learn that there is no "built-in" safety device that guards the integrity of a friendship other than trust. If that trust is somehow broken, our confidence in that relationship may end. We need to be discerning, to keep our hearts and minds open while still being cautious. This takes experience; it is only when we have a good character that others can trust us. When we are open to trusting others, we can live a life that is meaningful.

When we trust people, we are secure in the thought that they will not fail us.

Don't Hurry, Don't Worry, and Take Time to Smell the Flowers

Time is the key ingredient in commitment, empathy, and respect. It starts simply when we pause, look someone in the eyes, smile, and say hello. Then we take the time for them to answer. We do not look away, we do not looked rushed, we relax and appear to have all the time in the world to greet another. If we give the impression of having enough time, the person feels valued and respected.

Time Enough is Grace

In the 80s our church sponsored a Vietnamese family and my women's guild offered to help them with shopping and settling in. As a career woman, I was only able to offer two hours of my time.

I am by nature an impatient person, yet some gift of grace allowed me to spend those paltry two hours with these strangers in a way that fed their souls and mine. I was able to slow down, drink tea, play with the baby, and still have time to grocery shop and visit a garage sale with them.

Perhaps because I had so little time to offer, I fully committed myself to this family. They rewarded me with a graciousness and gratitude that overwhelmed me.

Anonymous

Time with Friends

"I want someone who respects me and wants to be with me, but who also cares enough about me to challenge me on some things and to offer me new ways of seeing things, ideas I hadn't come up with on my own...and, beyond that, someone who can communicate such things with gentle conviction, not with righteous and annoying insistence."

Bill Tammeus
The Kansas City Star

When we meet someone for the first time, we start building a link that can only be strengthened if we take proper time to listen and to make that person feel she has our full attention. No matter what other pressures one has, the impression must be that one is giving total attention and respect to the individual in front of us.

We create a sense of commitment in relationships by paying attention to little details, such as remembering someone's birthday or expressing appreciation for a job well done. When we do this, it is like building a chain where every link is forged with small attentions, remembrances, and the sharing of moments together. Time is the test by which we measure a relationship. When we forge strong links with time and attention, the relationship can weather many storms.

If the attentions we pay are a result of social conventions like Christmas and Valentine cards, we run the risk of artificiality if we are not communicating with true feeling. Those links need to be reinforced beyond the social conventions in order to be valued and appreciated.

Forming good relationships takes time every day. It is the continuity of our attention that shows that we care.

Bill Harsh, the human resources vice president of Hallmark cards in the 50s, had a unique ability to build relationships. He would take time to remember birthdays. He had the ability to look at people and remember the name of their children, birthdays, and other special occasions of a personal nature. Bill Harsh was a people person. He built genuine relationships with his sincere interest and loving concern for the people around him. Jack

We cannot hope to know or understand others if we do not spend enough time with them. Yet, with the immediacy of dealing with daily tasks, juggling time and responsibilities, it is easy to be spread too thin. When we stay on the surface, and do not explore our own depths and those of others, we become superficial.

The greatest gift we can give to ourselves and others is enough time. When we do not slow down, we endanger those qualities that are most precious: our physical, mental, and emotional health, our sense of perspective and relationship with others.

A Walk in the Park: Time to Be

It's break time. The coffee pot in the break room beckons. You hesitate. NO, today you will try something different.

Down the hall to the elevator, press G5, step into the parking garage, and out the door into the park. Your lungs expand; you feel yourself relax.

A little stiff at first, you find your stride and lope joyfully around the park. Wow! This is the life! The squirrels chase each other around a tree. You stop for a minute to admire a wonderful rhododendron bush. You greet someone else smiling her way around the path. You breathe.

Connected again, feeling more human, you head back to your desk.

TIME FOR REFLECTION

Are Virtual Relationships Real?

If you have an on-line relationship with someone, how does it compare to your relationships with people you have met in person?

What are the advantages and disadvantages of your on-line relationships?

Are you able to share more of yourself on-line than in person? If so, why?

Commitment

What are your priorities in terms of your time commitments?

Does the way you spend your time match your key values?

What changes do you need to make to feel good about your commitments?

Respect

Think of an example where you would have behaved differently if you had treated someone as they would have liked to be treated.

Describe a situation in which you found it difficult to show respect to someone?

If someone with a white cane is waiting to cross the street, how can you decide whether or not you should help?

Empathy

What is your experience of the difference between empathy and sympathy?

Think of a time you taught a child how to be empathic.

Have you every engaged in "e-truism"? How did you feel about this experience?

Think of a time when someone you just met felt "simpatico" to you.

I "feel" your pain.

Acceptance

Think of one of your flaws that a dear friend is able to accept and even celebrate.

How are you able to accept people whose culture is different from yours?

Trust

Describe relationships in your life that have different degrees of trust.

Think of people in your life you feel you can trust.

If you had a friendship that ended because trust was broken, how could you heal that wound?

Do you know someone you are not comfortable to be with because that person is not trusting? How do you deal with that person?

Time

When did you last take time to tell a special friend how much you care?

Share with someone else a dream of how you would like to spend time with others in a setting where time seems to stand still. Plan to make this dream come true.

Put this book down, put on your walking shoes, and head outdoors. Breathe. Smile. Think.

Unbroken Threads of Trust

"In the olden days, business records and accounts were kept in security bound ledgers. When the ledgers were bound but not cased in, they were dipped into a special bath where a unique pattern was transferred from the bath to the edges of the book. That was the security pattern. If anyone attempted to cut a page out and insert another page with faulty data, it could be immediately perceived as a fraud. So, the trust of the ledger had a built-in safety device."

Giacomo Spero

A precondition of good relationships

is mutual respect.

"Manners are the happy ways of doing things."

Ralph Waldo Emerson

From the simple statement of the Golden Rule, each culture has evolved a code of behaviors to help people live in harmony. These rules evolved over time and people learned to adopt them in order to be accepted in their society.

We react favorably to others when we are treated with respect, kindness, and sympathy. In return, we can be civil, polite or courteous depending on the time, place, and people with whom we are communicating.

We can be merely civil and avoid provoking or showing disrespect towards others. There is a certain coldness to this marginally correct behavior and usually we use it only if we want to distance ourselves from someone.

When we are polite, we are considerate and attentive to the feelings and needs of others. We hold doors open for people, say "please" and "thank you," don't push ahead in grocery lines, don't bump into people, and greet people when we meet them.

If we are courteous, we add to polite behaviors a dignity, polish, and graciousness that makes people feel special. We will still hold the door open, but we will do so with a smile and perhaps a greeting. When we see someone, we will not just say "hello" but smile warmly and perhaps ask about her family. These courtesies are social graces in practice.

"If a man be gracious and courteous to strangers, it shows he is a citizen of the world."

Francis Bacon
Philosopher

Expressing Social Graces

A precondition of good relationships is mutual respect: treating others as they would want to be treated, conveyed with sincerity. There are two main aspects of social graces. First, what is the message? Is it greetings, friendship, gratitude, apologies, or sympathy? Second, in what form will we communicate? Will we use the written word, our voice tone, body language, or the way we dress? The many combinations of these expressions make social graces an art form, one that reflects our personality.

The Message of Social Graces

There are untold rewards and satisfaction derived from making friends and maintaining the threads we weave into the social fabric of our lives. The various social graces and rules of etiquette that have evolved over time help us build the relationships that are important to us.

We practice social graces when we express the variety of feelings which convey how much we value the people in our lives.

Greetings: Smile and Say Hello

"Let a smile be your umbrella."

Kahal and Wheeler, songwriters

Greeting people in a welcoming way, with a smile, is the first step in showing respect. We might add to the warm greeting a smile and a sincere handshake. When we answer the phone with a cheerful voice, it conveys a smile to the caller and sets the right tone for positive communication.

Greeting someone with a smile smoothes the way. I learned this lesson well when attempting to buy a newspaper in Paris.

Early one morning I set out from my hotel in Paris to buy a newspaper. I approached the little newspaper stand, reached in my pocket for change, and asked the vendor for the Herald Tribune. She looked at me, with a smile and said, "Monsieur, we begin by saying, 'Bonjour'." There was a twinkle of reproach in her tone. I greeted her, and smiled. She gave me the paper. I realized then that it would be a gracious thing to begin my business transactions with a greeting and a smile.   Jack

"I work hard
to bring some light
into other people's lives.
I greet them
with a smile, I ask how
their day is going.
We are alive and
there are things that
are good about life."

Glenda Spellerberg

The gift of a smile costs us nothing and gives us instant feedback. The enthusiasm and friendliness of a smile can pave the way toward meaningful communication. But perhaps more important, if the smile is reflected back, then for an instant two people are emotionally linked and the ordinary moment is transcended into something special. In fact, scientists have discovered that when we smile our body chemistry changes. The feeling of happiness and well-being we experience is reflected by changes in our brain. More importantly, we have made a friend.

Thoughtfulness

Sometimes, it feels good just to let someone special know you are thinking of her. We can do this by sending a funny internet joke, phoning, or picking up a greeting card that catches our eye in a store.

There is a whole category of greeting cards called, "Thinking of You." Hallmark's first card in this line was a basket of pansies: pansies stand for thoughts. In the 50s, cards were created to satisfy a social custom called Secret Pals. Women would form a club so each person could secretly, by ballot, choose a friend to be remembered with cards. Throughout the year, each person would receive cards signed "Your Secret Pal." At the end of the year, there would be a party during which members would reveal themselves to their secret pal with a final card. The occasion was called "Revealing Secret Pal." This ritual was a way for people to say, "I am thinking of you," and "We belong to a circle of special friends."

Another way to express thoughtfulness is through random acts of kindness. A secret act of kindness can create a delicious sense of happiness in the giver as well as the receiver.

A secret act of kindness can create a delicious sense of happiness in the giver as well as the receiver.

When my two children were both under five years old, my husband was in the hospital suspected of having cancer. I came home from the hospital one day emotionally and physically exhausted. On the porch steps I saw a bouquet of flowers. My heart soared. Who could have sent them? The names of all my friends who might have been thoughtful enough ran through my mind. However, when I picked up the bouquet, I found they came from a business trying to start a bouquet-a-week service! I laughed! My joy was not diminished at all by this. The flowers helped me feel grateful for all my friends.

S.G. Hope

We all need kindness. When we experience an unexpected kindness, our heart soars in gratitude. We feel a sense of love and belonging.

Gratitude

Gratitude is being conscious of what is treasured. It is a natural impulse which, when shared, expresses warmth towards others and creates a bond between people. There are as many ways of expressing thanks as there are things to be grateful about. It is considered "polite" to say "thank you" for favors others do for us. However, if we express appreciation only as a social obligation, our insincerity dilutes the meaning. For this reason, gratitude other than the obligatory "thanks" is often perceived as more heartfelt if conveyed with a hug, a smile, a pat on the back, or the offer of a daisy from our garden.

"...one of my friends expects everything of the universe, and is disappointed when anything is less than the best....I begin at the other extreme, expecting nothing, and am always full of thanks for moderate goods."

Ralph Waldo Emerson

"The center of human nature is rooted in ten thousand ordinary acts of kindness that define our days."

Stephen Jay Gould

The best kind of gratitude is gratitude in action; to be aware of your own good fortune, and share it with others. Here are some examples of how we can express gratitude:

> **For life**,
>> by living with gratitude.
>
> **For happiness**,
>> by striving to make others happy.
>
> **For inspiration**,
>> by trying to inspire others.
>
> **For health**,
>> by caring for our bodies.
>
> **For friends**,
>> by being a good friend.

Expressing appreciation as a daily part of life not only brings us closer to others but helps us feel happy and content with our lives.

Other Expressions of Respect

We live with a rainbow of feelings and have many opportunities during the course of a day to strengthen our relationships by supporting people around us. There are no right or wrong ways to say, "I am sorry," "congratulations," or to express sympathy. It is the degree of sincerity with which we express our feelings, however clumsy, that counts. What we say must ring true to others if the meaning of what we say is to be appreciated.

When a friend died, we arranged a service of celebration for her with music and sincere thoughts shared by friends. It was a simple service but well thought out. At the end of the session, the chamber music quartet prepared to play its last few pieces. Suddenly, my friend's grandson stood up and walked to the front of the room. He was a disabled young man in several ways, but his warmth and sincerity shone forth as he said, "My grandmother was the best grandmother in the world. I miss her." After he sat down , there was a moment of profound silence as everyone felt for the first time the great loss my friend's death meant to us all. Many people silently cried.   S.G. Hope

The Style of Social Graces

The simple statements, "thank you" or "good morning" or "hello," can be expressed in an infinite variety of styles. There are formal, casual, informal, humorous, romantic, and many other ways to convey our thoughts. Style becomes an integral part of the message. The medium with which we express the thought, in fact, becomes the message.

An example of this fact is the manner in which we write, as this story suggests:

There was a plaque on the wall of an engraver's studio on Stoke-on-Trent, England, to remind the engraver of the qualities of a good engraving. The plaque said:

> **An engraving should be delicate but not weak;**
> **It should have vigor but not coarseness.**

We may think that an engraving is just an engraving. But this master craftsman was clear that his art was to convey the right feeling with every stroke of his chisel.

The Written Word

> ## *"Verba volent, scripta manent."*
>
> Latin saying

"Words fly, what is written remains forever." This Latin saying suggests how powerful the written word is as a means of communication. When we express our feelings in writing, our words have lasting meaning. Many people have a box for saving special letters which they may take pleasure in rereading periodically.

> *The medium with which we express the thought, in fact, becomes the message.*

In some parts of the world during the 1900s, the fine art of letter writing was an essential part of social graces. One woman described how, even as recently as the late 1950s, she was carefully taught the art of letter writing.

When I was twelve years old, my uncle in Ireland decided it was time for me to learn how to write a good letter. I was given a box of pink notepaper. My mother put a handkerchief soaked in perfume in the box so the pages would smell nice. I had to use a fountain pen, not a ballpoint pen which was considered too crude an instrument. Then, of course, there was the matter of the correct form of the letter: how to address the person, how to punctuate, how to end the letter. But it was also important to make the letter interesting. An appropriate topic had to be selected and written about in an engaging way. Finally, it was essential that the handwriting be pleasing and the letter laid out well.

It was an important art and my uncle took seriously his role as tutor. I would write him a letter on my lovely perfumed stationery. He would receive it in two or three weeks. With a red pen, he would correct my grammar, comment on the quality of the letter, and criticize my handwriting. His return letter, with mine enclosed, also contained a 20 pound note for encouragement.

I would write a new letter trying to improve my handwriting and my letter's charm, then wait impatiently for his response. S.G. Hope

This woman was being taught the importance of keeping in touch in a graceful and respectful way. The attention that went into her letters, the special paper, the pen, the layout, the interesting content, took a great deal of time and conveyed to the receiver how much she cared.

Has letter writing become obsolete? Certainly not. People still cherish the written word, still value having a sentiment they can hold onto and refer back to. People who lack the skill or time to adequately express their feelings in words may take advantage of the many greeting cards available which have messages for every occasion, taste, and kind of relationship.

People take advantage of the many greeting cards available which have messages for every occasion, taste, and kind of relationship.

*"Always do
what is right.
This will surprise
some people
and astonish
the rest."*

Mark Twain

With technological advances such as e-mail and cell phones, it is as easy to keep in touch with people around the world, as it is to stay in close communication with those we see every day. However, there is a different level of commitment and intimacy when a message comes in the form of a handwritten letter. This letter comes only to us. Our friend went to the trouble to find good paper, pen, and stamps. When we receive an e-mail, which many others in our friend's address book also received, we feel included in a social circle but we do not feel special.

Writing by hand slows us down and we have time to be more thoughtful. We can more carefully choose the words we feel are right. Many of us can type as fast as we think, so when we compose an e-mail message it is easy to write something we may regret later. It is time for an e-mail etiquette to help us pause and avoid mistakes that can occur when we rush.

On-line Manners

- Use language you would use in person.

- Use good grammar and punctuation.

- Share intimate and hurt feelings in person.

- Follow the Golden Rule.

- Remember that e-mail is a public medium. Be careful that what you say is not too private.

- Do not gossip or spread rumors.

- Do not harass people with too many e-mails.

- Be aware of the values of the other person when you send e-mail jokes, political cartoons, or religious stories.

Etiquette and Good Manners

> *"Good Manners is the art of making people comfortable in our presence."*
>
> Jonathan Swift

Over time, groups develop customs that help build a sense of community. These may relate to how we dress, how we greet, how we treat each other, and even how we eat. These social graces are a reflection of our respect for each other.

Some cultures have very strict rules governing dress, such as the shrouding of women in some Muslim countries. In western countries, however, the social rules for how to dress are more relaxed and often uninhibited. For example, American presidents may wear jeans and cowboy boots when they are relaxing. A good example of the American ethic in regard to dress etiquette is this advice:

You don't have to be glamorous; you just have to put your best foot forward. You need to be clean and presentable. You need to know how to walk and how to greet people. Then they will respond to you. Glenda Spellerberg

We will not be accepted if we dress too formally in an informal setting.

Yet there are rules which we follow in order to be accepted in different social settings. Just as we would not think of wearing our sweat pants to the office, neither would we dress too formally in an informal setting.

It would be hard to say what the general rules of good table manners are in a culture as diverse as ours. We eat hamburgers, fries, and pizza with our hands, but in a fancy restaurant we use our "party" manners. In some cultures, everyone reaches with their right hand into communal dishes, a practice we would find difficult to understand.

The general idea of good manners is to behave appropriately for the situation so that others feel comfortable. Yet fashions in

etiquette change. There is now a new wave of appreciation for the impression we give when we eat and dress in certain ways. Some people are once again looking for more formal rules of etiquette. Recently, etiquette specialists have begun to teach their clients how body language, eye contact, and handshakes, as well as correct forms of dress and table manners, can affect the way others perceive them.

Despite the informality and diversity of our culture, we are still aware of the importance of social rules in helping us to get along and be accepted.

Body language, eye contact, handshakes, as well as correct forms of dress can affect the way others perceive them.

Celebrations and Traditions

Traditions create a sense of continuity and a feeling of being a part of our family, neighborhood, city, and country. They help build memories which bridge our past with the present. Celebrations often become traditions and help us integrate into our communities.

For example, Harvest Thanksgiving feasts are celebrated in many countries to show gratitude for the bounty of nature and the hard work of the farmers who grow our food. In the United States, this day of gratitude is set aside to honor our common heritage.

On a more personal note, we may celebrate a member of a group for outstanding accomplishment. To honor one person with special recognition makes the whole group feel more cohesive. Recently, the head of a company was honored on his 80th birthday. An elegant album was provided as a way to gather people's expression of appreciation. It brought everyone together as they thought about this man, his impact on their lives, and how grateful they were that they knew him.

Family traditions and celebrations can begin as routines we set up for ourselves and our children. Parents will often turn an everyday event like bedtime into a ritual that calms the children and gives them a sense of security. A family may create celebrations around special events. These become the markers that say to a child, "I belong to the Smith family and Dad makes pancakes every Sunday."

In some neighborhoods, traditional summer block parties give the adults and children an opportunity to meet each other and reinforce relationships. Many cities host annual celebrations which promote pride and become traditions, such as an annual mayor's Christmas tree lighting, summer festival, or a day set aside to honor special people for outstanding accomplishments.

The circle of life is honored by many occasions: the birth of a baby, graduation, marriage, and death are common occasions for celebrations of connection and life. Many people no longer talk about funerals but rather "Celebrations of Life" when a loved one dies. At this time we celebrate the life of a person and remember how much that person meant to the community. But it is also time for us to reflect on our own life, on what we have done, and what we feel we have yet to do.

At whatever level they take place, our celebrations and traditions are essential parts of our lives that create memories and give us a sense of continuity.

Telegraphing Our Feelings

We have described the medium and the message and how they are totally integrated in conveying our feelings. We each carry within ourselves an integrated medium and message. In other words, people will react to how we are dressed, our facial expressions, the way we sit, and the tone of our voice, as much as to what we are trying to say. It is as if we are actually telegraphing a message with added meaning.

The ways we talk, dress, eat, and greet others may vary, but when we are comfortable with social graces, we are able to deal with different social situations with natural ease and confidence. In return, people will feel comfortable with us and we will have a positive experience with our relationships.

Dad makes pancakes every Sunday.

TIME FOR REFLECTION

Social Graces

When are you merely civil instead of polite?

When are you courteous?

Smile and Say Hello

Observe the power of a friendly smile and a cheery hello.

Thoughtfulness

Think of a time you performed a random act of kindness.

Think of a time someone was kind to you unexpectedly.

The Written Word

When, if ever, do you prefer "snail mail" to e-mail?

What do each of these mediums add to your life?

Apology

"Give me strength to be the first to tender the healing word and the renewal of friendship, that the bonds of amity and the flow of charity may be strengthened."

Cecil Hunt

Gratitude

Think of someone deserving of your gratitude whom you have taken for granted?

Recall an experience when a bouquet of flowers helped erase a bad feeling.

Traditions and Celebrations

What are your favorite traditions and celebrations?

Which traditions and celebrations are part of your family's heritage?

Which personal celebrations turned into traditions?

Etiquette

Remember a time you committed a serious breach of etiquette that embarrassed you, but that now makes you laugh.

> *"Half the world is composed of people who have something to say and can't, and the other half who have nothing to say and keep on saying it."*
>
> Robert Frost
> American Poet

PASSION FOR KNOWLEDGE

PASSION FOR KNOWLEDGE

*"A man's mind may be likened to a garden,
which may be intelligently cultivated
or allowed to run wild."*

Giacomo Spero

The one quality in an astronaut more powerful than any other is curiosity. They have to get to someplace no one has ever been to before.

John Glenn, astronaut

From the beginning of time we have been asking ourselves questions about Mars. In 2004, we witnessed the elation of NASA scientists as they watched their craft land on Mars, 141 million miles away. Their reward was to witness the craft doing the job it was designed to do. Now their curiosity is whetted again. What will they learn? What will the pictures reveal? What will be the consequences of the new discovery?

The thirst for knowledge is unquenchable. Learning begins simply with the pleasure and excitement of our own personal discoveries. As children, we explore and challenge ourselves to have mastery over our small part of the world. The child is proud to say, "I CAN DO IT! I AM AMAZING!" We nurture this passion for exploration and mastery throughout our lives. Imagine a grandmother who gets her first computer at age 80 saying, "I DID IT!" when she successfully sends her first e-mail. Her use of this new technology has expanded her vision and given her the pleasure of accomplishment. Challenging oneself in this way is like reliving childhood, when life is new and exciting every day.

Curiosity is the spark that increases our passion for knowledge. It makes us want to climb another mountain to see the valley and beyond. Our exhilaration compels us to go up the rough path one step at a time and over the boulders. When we get to the top what will we see? Another mountain? Another challenge?

Being curious stimulates our thinking. Passion for knowledge fuels our determination to reach beyond the present. It helps us to overcome momentary setbacks and keeps us focused so we may achieve what we may never have thought possible. Only when our vision is expanded by knowledge can our dreams become reality.

"Do the things you like doing. I made my living doing something I would have done for nothing. I know not everyone can do that. But find time in your day to do what you love."

Buck O'Neil
Baseball Legend

Set long and short-term attainable goals. Reach for the stars if you care to, but have a vehicle to get there. That vehicle is usually knowledge. A person who is knowledgeable understands the way to get to their goal.   Mike Dearing

If age is a state of mind, then by fueling our curiosity we can keep on learning and never grow "old." Even when our lives undergo extraordinary changes, we are sustained by the anticipation of a new day.

The words of Sir Winston Churchill seem appropriate here. In 1943 he said, *"The empires of the future are the empires of the mind."*

How Curious Are You?

1. Do you wake up in the morning excited about what the day might bring?

2. Do you find even the familiar things in life fascinating?

3. Do you seek as much information as you can about a new situation or ideas?

4. Do you look for new challenging opportunities?

5. Are you as playful and spontaneous as you were as a child?

6. Can you lose track of time when you are involved in an activity?

7. Do your friends seek you out to help them get perspective on things?

8. Do you feel that you understand yourself well?

9. Are you open minded enough to look at all sides of an issue and weigh the evidence?

10. Can you learn as much from your mistakes as from your successes?

11. Are you comfortable with your ability to deal with whatever life has in store for you?

Age is a quality of mind

If you have left your dreams behind,

If hope is lost,

If you no longer look ahead,

If ambitions' fires are dead,

Then, you are old.

Cicelia Payne-Grove
Age 101

When we get to the top, what will we see?

CURIOSITY: The Continuing Quest For Knowledge

"Dear Friends, open the saucers of your ears,
so that with the ladle of my science, I can pour into you
the soup of my knowledge."

Italian Baroque Expression

"The primary purpose of a liberal education is to make one's mind a pleasant place in which to spend one's leisure."

Sidney J. Harris

I t may seem that we are motivated primarily by our basic needs for water, food, shelter, comfort, relationships, and procreation. However, curiosity is the engine that drives people to seek the knowledge that can lead to the satisfaction of our basic needs.

We now have unlimited resources to draw upon in our drive to satisfy our curiosity. Libraries are connected around the world and knowledge has multiplied. There are classes and workshops for every imaginable interest from fly-fishing, to book binding, to meditation. Our quest for knowledge can take us wherever our curiosity leads us. Curiosity enables us to obtain the knowledge we need in order to have self-determination, power, and meaning in our life.

Knowledge as Power

The books about faraway wonders and exciting adventures, which we discover as children, fire our imagination and spark our curiosity to seek new horizons. The knowledge we gain can become a source of power, not an end in itself. It is the means by which we direct the life we choose. With a passion for knowledge we get an intense drive to discover and understand the changes that are occurring around us. **Knowledge gives us the power to do what we want to do.**

There was a time when the privileged elite used the power of knowledge to control people.

In ancient Egypt, the Pharaoh ruled with absolute power which was tempered only by the high priests. Together, they used the science of the day to predict and control the outcome of crucial events. One of the primary bases of their power was their ability to accurately predict the annual flooding of the Nile.

Make one's mind a pleasant place in which to spend one's leisure.

The fertile banks and the delta of the river Nile depended on the regular yearly flood and the deposit of silt. Nilometers, descending staircases leading down into the river, were used to measure the depth of the rising water over the last 1,000 miles upstream. These measurements enabled the priests to predict the amount of flood water that could be expected in the fertile Delta. A good flood would mean bountiful silt and good crops. In these years, the Pharaoh could increase taxes. A prediction of a dry year would prompt the priests to consider the amount of offerings they needed to pacify the God Nile. So the elite had it both ways, whether there was a drought or a flood, the offerings or taxes would keep full the coffers of the Pharaoh and the high priests.

The privilege of knowledge allowed the rulers of the world to maintain absolute power until the advent of a new technology in 15th century Germany. At that time, Gutenburg invented printing with moveable type. The balance of power was forever changed because the printing press made mass production of books possible. The dissemination of knowledge led to a challenge to the absolute power which had been concentrated in the hands of the few. From then on, dams could not be built high enough to contain the enormous pressure of the collective aspirations of the newly empowered people. For awhile, the elite did contain the emerging power of this flood of knowledge through the constraints of force and censorship. The vast number of censored books in the Vatican Library are a reminder of this time.

Knowledge to me is not a commodity you can buy, it is really free. I can access knowledge and information at any time. And I do.
Vicki Franklin

If we have a passion for knowledge, we have a key to understanding the world around us, especially these days when the computer multiplies our resources and extends them beyond

The balance of power was forever changed.

national borders. We are bombarded by new scientific applications and the increasing spread of new ideas every day. The electronic brain, combined with our human brain, enables us to elevate our thinking to new heights. Knowledge begets more knowledge.

Literacy as a Key to Knowledge and Self-determination

"Knowledge will be the key resource of the Next Society...Knowledge workers will be the dominant group in the workforce."

Peter Drucker

A modern example of the power of literacy is the story of the benevolent Turkish dictator Kemal Ataturk. After World War I, he brought Turkey into the modern era with several remarkable changes. At the time, texts were read from right to left and printing required a laborious hand setting process. Ataturk dictated that the Turkish language be adapted to the phonetics of the Roman alphabet. This transformation made it possible for Turkey to take advantage of western technology to automate and accelerate the introduction of textbooks and literature. He then made universal education available and mandatory. It was in large part this availability of knowledge that enabled Turkey to rise from the ashes of the old Ottoman empire as a new modern republic.

Today, success in life requires literacy, which is essential to our pursuit of knowledge.

Knowledge is so crucial to self-determination of individuals and nations that the United Nations Convention on the Rights of the Child and the U.N. Millennium Development Goals both target education. In the U.N. Millennium Development Goals, universal primary education for boys and girls is second only to the goal of eradicating extreme poverty and hunger.

Interdisciplinary Studies Valued

Living proof that knowledge is power, many leverage their wealth to effect radical reforms in public education. One such person is Melinda Gates, who in 1999 gave $20 million to Duke University. The money is earmarked to encourage intellectual curiosity by promoting interdisciplinary studies (the study of several disciplines at once).

Adapted from a report in
Trend Letter, 1999

While these global institutions advocate literacy as a necessity for children, it is only when each country makes education its priority that changes are possible. For example, even a nation as advanced as the United States has recently passed an initiative called, *"No Child Left Behind."*

At the local level, each community must adapt this educational mandate to its own culture. Progress will only occur when teachers and parents are committed to providing the time and initiative to translate the goal of universal literacy into reality.

One person in our community who has this commitment is Vicki Franklin. She left her corporate position and started a business tutoring children in the public schools. Her passion is not just to help children become literate, but to instill in them a passion for learning. She feels strongly that mentoring the whole child can help bridge the cultural obstacles to learning often experienced by an African American child.

A person whose first learning experiences are unpleasant or difficult will miss the opportunities available to those who have acquired curiosity and a love of learning. Furthermore, they will not appreciate the value of knowledge in making their life more meaningful. The personal relationships Vicki has nurtured with her students help her identify and correct that which inhibits their progress, but more importantly, she is able to inspire her students to model her passion for knowledge.

New Knowledge is Based on the Old

The more we know, the more we want to know, which is one of the most exciting aspects of our lives. So, new discoveries are built on the shoulders of those who preceded us. This is true in science as well as in the humanities. What we learn quickly becomes outdated as new discoveries are added to our store of knowledge. What better way to appreciate what we have today than by comparing it with the classics and science of the past. Should our field of interest begin to bog down, we can rekindle our inspiration and find new direction by revisiting the timeless wisdom of the past. Charles Gusewelle, whose newspaper column inspires many, gets his inspiration from the classic writers:

> *"Information expands as it is used. It's as transportable as the speed of light. Above all, it leaks; it has an inherent tendency to leak."*
>
> Harlan Cleveland
> Futurist

What I find most necessary from time to time, is to restore my belief in the importance of writing and the power of words. To do that I go back to the classics, to the modern classics, to people whose writing I grew up on. I am reading to understand and to be moved by their achievement. I read them for inspiration.

Likewise in the scientific world, researchers find inspiration in the theories of the scientific classics. For example, Einstein's Theory of Relativity, which was published about 100 years ago, continues to provide inspiration for new technology as well as excitement in unraveling the mysteries of the universe.

The New Elite – a 21st Century Paradox

Computer technology has put ever-increasing sources of knowledge at our fingertips. However, it is said that the computer allows access to only one inch of the vast ocean of knowledge that is available. We can all get to know a little about a lot. Yet new discoveries are still the domain of a few because of the length of time required to validate a discovery that will be the seed of new scientific applications.

An example is the discovery in the 1950s of the spiral model/double helix structure of DNA by research biologists Watson and Crick. Their research expanded the scope of molecular biology and genetics. Today, biotechnology and related fields of science bring to us a unique understanding of how life is formed. Numerous applications are constantly emerging to the benefit of mankind. Even the artistic community has been inspired by the image of the double helix.

This example, however, suggests that our lives are being shaped by an emerging elite class of scientists whose discoveries will determine the future direction of society. These scientists, whose life work is basic research, and the creation of applications for their new discoveries, are as powerful an elite as the old rulers and aristocracy. What follows their work is an explosion of innovations that will affect every aspect of our lives. Do we know enough about genetics to make an informed decision about the ethical consequences of genetic engineering? Can we really understand the new advances in computer science? Do we need to?

Unforeseen Success

Inventors' visions may turn out to be wrong because they may succeed in unforeseen ways. *"Visionaries get things wrong because they concentrate too much on the technology, and fail to take into account the way it is shaped by social forces as it spreads."*

The Economist
March 13, 2004

The one comforting thought about this emerging elite is that it is a meritocracy based on the abilities and achievements of individuals. In a country that has universal access to education, anyone who is determined and has the ability to learn can become a part of this technocracy. On the one hand, technology is a tool that helps expand our knowledge and enhance our lives. On the other hand, it can raise serious ethical questions. Progress may be inhibited because the magnitude of change resulting from this emerging research creates fear of the unknown. This fear is often politicized by some segments of society whose beliefs are challenged by the new discoveries. Others, however, feel that it is possible to balance the moral imperative of social responsibility with scientific progress.

"Everything in life is a hobby if you enjoy it."

Rose Stolowy

Curiosity Creates Meaning

For many people a meaningful life requires a passion for learning. Both Dr. Friesen and Dr. Neaves feel that curiosity and creativity are essential to a good life. Dr. Neaves's advice to a young person about how to live a meaningful life is as follows:

Always be mentally engaged in an enterprise that transcends normal daily concerns: something that has meaning and persists long after one's demise.

Rose Stolowy gives similar advice. Boredom is just not part of her vocabulary; there is so much to learn. Now in her 90s she is deepening her understanding of her faith by reading the English translations of Hebrew texts she did not have the time to read before. She uses the computer to communicate with her grandchildren, and she enjoys many hobbies. For Rose, *"Everything in life is a hobby if you enjoy it."*

The Zigs and Zags of Learning

"Most of the things worth doing in the world had been declared impossible before they were done."

Louis Brandeis

The gold of knowledge is ours to take. But how much can we carry away?

The learning curve can be compared to a series of zigs and zags. Imagine a graph, with the horizontal axis representing our lifeline, and the vertical one illustrating our developing knowledge and level of skill. As we acquire and apply knowledge, we have experiences that can have positive or negative outcomes. The positive outcomes move us upward and forward. When we encounter a setback, and understand the reason for it, we are motivated to try again. As we plot these progressions and regressions, it becomes clear that the path of our learning has an upward trend with minor interruptions which make the trajectory look like the teeth of a giant saw. When our learning creates a negative result, the line zags down. When it has a positive result, the line zigs up. Hopefully, no zag is deep enough to drastically alter our progress.

These ups and downs add richness and spice to our lives. It is important to try new things that really challenge us. It can be humbling to begin at the beginning with some new skill; to experience again, as an adult, the frustration, challenges and exhilaration of learning. But this is what stimulates our brain and makes us feel new again.

In book learning, I am very quick. So it was a shock for me to learn that I am a very slow learner when it comes to physical things. I discovered this when I was 45 years old and decided to follow a childhood dream of taking tap dancing lessons. I was fairly good at picking up the rhythm of a particular step, but I was all left feet when I had to synchronize two steps. It was very frustrating, but gave me a new appreciation of people who are slower than I am to grasp abstract concepts. My final humiliation came on the night of the big recital. Our little troop ended our dance sequence, and shuffled off to Buffalo – but they went left, and I, alone, shuffled off right! S.G. Hope

Open Sesame

The vast and rich complexity of knowledge available to us can be compared to the Ali Baba cave loaded with jewels and gold. The gold of knowledge is ours to take. But how much can we carry away? It is not possible for one person to know everything. The sheer magnitude of ideas we are exposed to can be overwhelming. We can know only a little about some things, or a lot about a few things. Therefore, when we say the magic words "Open Sesame" and venture into the vault of treasures, we need to select carefully. We need to make choices that enhance our understanding, but not at the expense of our values.

New Skills Enhance Old Talents

I took piano lessons from two kinds of teachers at the same time.

Sixty years ago I thought I knew everything; now I know nothing; education is a progressive discovery of our own ignorance.

Will Durant

When we learn a new skill, whether to replace or rejuvenate an old one, we add a new dimension to our repertoire. A musician will delight in many different kinds of music.

Yo Yo Ma, the famous classical cellist, also plays jazz, blue grass, and the tango. An amateur pianist, Dr. Friesen is so passionate about developing his musical skills that he studies continuously.

In my avid search for learning I even took piano lessons from two kinds of teachers at the same time. One was Mrs. Wilson, who was an absolute perfectionist for classical music, and the other was a man who taught me a real progressive jazz. He was the best jazz piano player I ever heard.

"Creative people are compelled by their passion to find new ways of expressing their talent," says Dr. Friesen. They continue to experiment to satisfy their creative urge. When we have a passion for knowledge, there is no limit to where our curiosity may take us.

Jim Cathcart, author of **The Acorn Principle**, said, *"When we do something the same way each time, it narrows our vision and limits our ability to adjust to unforeseen circumstances."* Trying a new skill is like opening up the gates of creativity to a new vision.

Hidden Treasures

Learning does not just mean satisfying curiosity, but also seeing and understanding something at a deeper level. There is a world of beauty within our grasp, waiting to be discovered. On our walk through a park, we may notice for the first time a particularly lovely flower etched by a ray of light, or the way the light plays off the cascading water in the fountain. When we leave that park, we will feel more peace.

We can enhance the meaning in our life when we appreciate things at a deeper level. The former curator of photography at the Museum of Modern Art, Edward Steichen, set up a camera in front of his bedroom window. He took a photo of the same tree every day and observed the changes caused by different light, seasons, and growth. Observing this familiar object through its daily changes, deepened and enhanced his appreciation of its beauty.

My father used to tell me that when you visit a city for the first time, you can enjoy it more if you walk or ride in a horse and buggy. Years ago, on a business trip to New York City, I found myself with plenty of time before my next meeting.

I decided to take a horse and buggy to the appointment at the Cooper-Hewitt National Design Museum, which was up Madison Avenue about 40 blocks from my hotel. At first, the buggy driver was hesitant. He wanted to take me around the

I took a horse and buggy to the appointment.

park! But I insisted that I wanted to go up the Avenue. I sat in the back of the carriage enjoying the window displays and architecture. The gentle pace of the horse allowed me time to really see the glories of Madison Avenue and to record my impressions.

Jack

When we slow down, when we look deeply, when we listen attentively, the richness of the world has a chance to unfold around us and allows us to capture many special moments in everyday life.

What Limits our Passion for Knowledge?

In his book, ***The Art of Living***, Wilfred A. Peterson advised that staying young depends on being youthful in our minds, hearts, and spirits.

… by forcing your mind out of old ruts. Remember that beaten paths are for beaten men. See new places, read new books, try new hobbies. Increase the depth of your life…Stay young by remaining flexible, adaptable and open minded. Do not permit your mental arteries to harden.

Mr. Peterson would not make excuses for the fact that as we grow older, we may find some types of learning more difficult. A reviewer wrote this reply:

Yes, Mr. Peterson, we agree that we should not permit our mental arteries to harden, but as for our physical arteries, that's a different matter. They will harden whether we permit them to or not.

Will this dampen our love of learning? Not likely! There are numerous devices out there clamoring for attention, claiming they can minimize the effects of diminished hearing, sight, and an unbelievable number of other functions. We just have to know where to find them, and we do.

In my class, the students, whose average age is 75, sport hearing aides, walking canes, and haul their back rests with them. They rarely miss a class. They will shyly admit to plugged arteries now and then, but not to plugged minds – never.

Miriam McCartney

> *"He who would learn to fly one day must first learn to stand and walk and run and climb and dance: one cannot fly into flying."*
>
> Friedrich Wilhelm Nietzche
> German Philosopher

Limitations Can Become the Challenge That Spurs Our Creativity

A local artist, Gaby Mountain, has adopted new mediums as her physical abilities and stamina have evolved. She started her career by creating images in stone and marble, then moved to wood, pounded metals, mosaics, and finally, in her 70s, taught herself to weave. Each new medium inspired her to learn a new technique and enabled her to continue creating. She has found new passion for her art with each change.

When we remain curious and keep learning, we find ways to sidestep our limitations and handicaps and continue to discover a passion for life.

"It is not a bad practice for a person of many years to die with a child's heart."

Carl Sandburg

Being Open to Life

The quest for knowledge can be as simple as getting up each morning with an eager heart, curious about what the day may bring. When we can appreciate ordinary things in a new way, life can be full of surprises. We may challenge ourselves to learn a new skill or perfect an old one. We may spend hours reading or searching the web for information. Whatever our viewpoint, curiosity enriches our lives and keeps us involved in the events that affect us.

"Be brave enough to live life creatively. The creative is the place where no one else has ever been. You have to leave the city of your comfort and go into the wilderness of your intuition. You can't get there by bus, only by hard work and risk and by not quite knowing what you're doing. What you'll discover will be wonderful. What you'll discover will be yourself."

Alan Alda

"One thing life taught me: if you are interested, you never have to look for new interests. They come to you. When you are genuinely interested in one thing, it will always lead to something else."

Eleanor Roosevelt

Building Our Knowledge Reserves

Pablo Casals, the legendary cellist, was considered a prodigy as a teenager. He was tutored along with the Crown Prince of Spain. Every week the boys were taken to the Prado museum in Madrid and required to write a critical essay about what they had observed. When young Pablo complained about this to the tutor, he was told, "You will be a famous musician one day and you will need to know more than music in order to live a full life outside of your profession."

Pablo Casals was encouraged by an enlightened tutor to expand his interests beyond his formidable talent for the cello. As parents, we are often amazed at the natural talents of our children. We are thrilled with the gift of a beautiful watercolor signed by our 5 year old. So much natural talent. Yet later, when that 5 year old is a college graduate, we are sad that he seems to have forgotten this natural gift and no longer does watercolors.

We need to become young again.

Most of us have memories of childhood interests and innate gifts that we lost or set aside as we became adults in order to deal with the necessities of making a living. Now, as we reach middle age and are more financially secure, we might rediscover and redevelop these talents. To do this, we need to become innocent again; we need to be open, as we were as children, to the feeling that we can do anything.

We have within us reserves of talents we can build on to bring new meaning to our lives. We need only to spark again the innate curiosity we have that has been overshadowed by the reality and limitations within which we felt compelled to live. This is the time to break that glass ceiling of our imagined limitations and find the hidden treasures we left behind in childhood.

TIME FOR REFLECTION

Knowledge as Power

Describe how the pursuit of knowledge has enriched your life.

Has your discovery of new knowledge ever challenged your core values?

Relying on Experts

What are those issues that you feel inadequate to make an informed decision about?

Your Zigs and Zags

Think of a time your downward zags motivated you to try again.

Who Rules? You or Your Tools?

In what way is your lifestyle affected by new technological applications (palm pilot, digital camera, DVD, computer games, etc.)?

Your Hidden Treasures

Reflect for a moment on the hidden treasures you have found in something familiar.

Limitations Can Spur Creativity

Think of ways in which your limitations have compelled you to look at your life and talents in a new way.

Building Our Knowledge Reserves

Revisit the innocence of your childhood, the time before you knew you could not do things. Try again those creative activities that brought you joy.

> *"This world of ours is a new world, in which the unit of knowledge, the nature of human communities, the order of society, the order of ideas, the very notions of society and culture have changed and will not return to what they have been in the past. What is new is new, not because it has never been there before, but because it has changed in quality."*
>
> Robert Oppenheimer
> Physicist

What will I be when I grow up?

"I would like to be remembered for what I did for others rather than what I did for myself."

James E. Stowers

From the moment we are born, our family and friends gaze on us in wonder and ponder what we will make of our lives. In fact, if we think about it, our whole life seems to be about answering the question, "What will I be when I grow up?" Remember?

- When you were eight you may have been proud to claim, "When I grow up I want to be a fireman, a teacher, a doctor, a policeman, or a mechanic."

- When you were eighteen, the relatives peered at you intently over the Thanksgiving turkey and asked, "What are you going to study in college?" You hadn't a clue, but you gamely answered: accounting, premed, law, or science.

- At your wedding, the in-laws fixed you with a firm look and asked what your career plans were. You were just trying to earn a living and so you put a good face on things by saying, "I've got excellent prospects at ABC insurance company" or "I'm assured of a position at XYZ for an internship."

- At your 20th high school reunion, you looked nervously around at the others, too old to be your high school buddies, and wondered if they were doing better than you were.

- Later, at the height of your career, you may ask yourself, "What shall I do with the rest of my life?"

> *"The creative act thrives in an environment of mutual stimulation feedback and constructive criticism in a community of creativity."*
>
> William T. Brady

By mid-life, if we are fortunate, all of our hard work will have paid off. We now have a comfortable place to live, a decent car, and enough money for more than life's basics. If we have managed our finances for the long term, we may even see the possibility of retirement while we are still healthy enough to enjoy it. We have worked hard and learned much.

So, now what are we going to do with the rest of our life? More of the same? Work to earn money so we can enjoy ourselves? Spend more time on the golf course? Go to more out-of-state football games? Buy a bigger house with walk-in closets? Travel? All these things can bring us contentment.

However, some of us may feel there has got to be more to this life. As we look back, we realize **how much our success has depended on the support of other people**. We become aware that we are now in a position to help others achieve their dreams by passing along the knowledge we have acquired.

Pepiniere: Nurturing the Seeds of Life

The French use the word "pepiniere" to mean growing seeds (pepin) in a protected environment. Pepiniere can apply not just to raising flowers and plants, but also to carefully raising children until they are strong enough to fare for themselves.

Investing in our children is like planting a tree. Like an acorn, even the smallest investment in our children holds great promise, awaiting only time, nourishment and the right place to grow. It requires patience to nurture a child to have a passion for learning. The results don't spring up overnight. Those who look for growth too quickly may cause their sprouts to wither and die, while those who allow time for strong roots to form will almost certainly see their children mature and flourish.

Children should be challenged to develop freedom of thought and expression. They need to learn to think for themselves. It is important to expose a child to a variety of ideas, using education to promote curiosity and creativity. It does a child no favor to narrow his focus to career preparation too early in life.

Before graduating from the gymnasium (high school), I went to my father and said, "I would like to take accounting so I can help you in your business." My dad was touched by my thoughtfulness, but because he recognized my true aptitude, he said, "I can teach you the principles of accounting in 48 hours. Take the time you need to study the classics. They will be the springboard to a broader perspective and enrich your life." That was the prophecy of my father. I owe him a lot for that advice, which helped me to choose what eventually became the foundation of my future careers.

Jack

It does a child no favor to narrow his focus to career preparation too early in life.

By the time most American children reach the age of eight they are being carefully nurtured in a protected environment by many adults and institutions. At first, it is our family that provides us with what we need to grow. Many of us have been fortunate enough to have had grandparents or a special relative in our lives. They enriched us with their support and unique experiences. A grandparent's stories of the past can make history come alive. Having lived through three or four generations, they can be the bridge that gives a child a unique perspective on the past and, therefore, a better understanding of the present.

Sometimes it is the older people in the neighborhood who act as grandparents. In our neighborhood, it was an older couple we called Aunt Helen and Uncle Cuddy. The affection and care this dear couple gave our children added to their appreciation for life beyond what we parents could give them. Aunt Helen instilled in the children a love of flowers. Uncle Cuddy was an avid reader. He shared some of the histories he read with an excitement that held the attention of the children for hours on end. Jack

An "elder" can be any person who helps someone younger discover and enjoy new experiences: how to bake cookies, set a table, throw a football, or plant flowers. To a child, anyone older is old, so a teenager can be an "elder" to a younger child by showing respect and care: teaching their young neighbors how to play ball, watching over them on Halloween nights, and just being a good buddy. In a good neighborhood, each person has some feeling of responsibility for the children on her block.

By the time a young person reaches college age, they have been helped and influenced by many people outside their home. One such person, a school teacher, can be a phenomenal influence over a career spanning thirty or forty years. The wonderful book, **Goodbye, Mr. Chips**, by James Hilton, makes us think about the enormous influence one person's dedication can have on so many. Because they have the ability to inspire, remarkable teachers can be springboards to their students' future success. Not every student can be reached by a teacher, but those who are often acknowledge the debt owed.

It is said that it takes a village to grow a child. When a young person grows up to be a productive and happy member of society, we all benefit from our investment of time and caring.

Volunteering and Mentoring

We owe a debt of gratitude to the many people who volunteer their time and skill to enrich the lives of children: scout leaders, soccer coaches, Sunday school teachers, and youth group leaders, among others. These adults give freely of their knowledge, skills, and time to enrich others, and in the end they enrich themselves.

One year, our family traveled to Indiana when the children were 8, 10, and 12. We stayed in a beautiful park near Indianapolis. Early in the morning, a park ranger took us for a walk in the woods and told us about the trees and how to identify them by their bark and leaves.

Not every student can be reached by a teacher.

He taught us how to look deeply at the environment. It was a most beautiful three hours that appealed to the whole family. The forester who guided us around was a volunteer in his 70s. While he was showing us how to look at and appreciate nature, he was also renewing his own passion for the trees. Jack

There are many ways to share our time and skills with others. We can help by building a house for Habitat for Humanity, or working in a soup kitchen, or raking leaves for the older couple next door, or leading a youth group. Or, we can volunteer our professional skills to help others succeed.

Tina Sprinkle, a personal trainer, volunteered to set up a physical fitness program at a shelter for battered women. Her goal is to give these women a feeling of empowerment by getting fit and understanding their bodies. This dedication gives special meaning to her life. She shares not just her professional skill, but also her personal experience in the value of exercise in creating a sense of personal power.

There are opportunities for people to volunteer to teach their skills with computers. When teenagers help older persons who need to learn those skills, they become **reverse mentors**. This dedication helps young people develop emotional maturity by finding satisfaction in being useful to others. Mentoring and other kinds of volunteering encourage young people to become self-reliant, confident, and involved.

Teenagers can become reverse mentors.

Nurture Supports Nature

"If you had access to lots of resources, if mentors were available to you, if your young life was filled with love, coaching, support, encouragement, and success in overcoming obstacles, then your background is considered enriched. That means you had a good foundation on which to build your self-esteem. You had a head start in most situations, and you experienced very little self-doubt compared to most other people."

Jim Cathcart
Author

Passing the Baton: The Riches of Mentorship

Many of us have been fortunate to have had a parent, a teacher, or a friend who gave us the encouragement, advice, and knowledge we needed to win the first leg of our relay race. When we start a new career, we often look for a mentor. We choose someone we trust who can inspire us to do more than we think we are capable of achieving. When we mentor someone and use the wealth of our knowledge and experience, it is like passing the baton to him so he may continue the race successfully.

Mentoring begins with trust that grows into stronger ties over time. This relationship enriches the giver and the receiver because the process of mentoring requires the giving of oneself freely. Both are the beneficiaries of this kind of sharing and are enriched by it.

Dr. Friesen, who is in his 80s, still teaches first- and second-year medical students. He wants to get them when they are young and *"while they still have that luster in their eyes and enthusiasm."* His focus now is not on the science of medicine, but on the importance of medicine to society, social concerns, and medical ethics. These are the ideas he has accumulated from his years of studying philosophy, one of his hobbies. These young people are fortunate to have access to a man who not only can teach them, but mentor them with his passion for learning and life.

Dedicated people enjoy sharing their skills and experience. In these difficult times, more than ever, there is a need to inspire youth with our key values.

A successful business man, John Wurst, described how his greatest joy of the week was his mentoring session with a young man in the local elementary school. They meet for an hour to talk, go over homework, or just "hang out." Mr. Wurst is not acting like a tutor, teaching anything specific. He is more of an inspiration for a boy who is in need of someone to support his self-confidence and self-esteem. As a mentor, Mr. Wurst feels it is

"Because you believe in me, I believe in me."

Anonyous

important for him to inspire with **BLT**: I **Believe** that I will persevere in helping;
We will **Like** each other; we **Trust** each other.

The influence of a caring mentor on a young person during the critical
formative years can last a lifetime. One grateful person thanked her mentor this way:

> *"You gave us something precious and rare...*
> *the joy, the passion and the spirit of curiosity.*
> *For all these gifts, we thank you."*

The Gift of Sharing Knowledge

To share our ideas with the people

of the future gives them legs.

Giacomo Spero

By the time we are ready for our 20th high school reunion, it is likely that most
of us are hitting our stride in our chosen field. We know our strengths and use them
effectively. We have established a satisfactory social network. Our family life seems to
work well. However, most of us lead fairly self-centered lives at this time, judging our
self-worth by what we have accomplished and accumulated.

If we have reached middle age and are wondering, "Is there more to life?" we
are probably seeking something beyond the material *good life*. We experience life as
good when we have an opportunity to invest in ourselves, to try things out, and learn
new things. Yet what good is it to have phenomenal gifts if they cannot be used to help
others?

It is the application of knowledge that is the important factor, not the
accumulation of knowledge. It is the fulfillment of a lifetime when we can give back
something more valuable than money. When we share our knowledge, it is like
passing the baton to someone else.

The best gift

is the gift

of oneself.

It Is in Sharing Our Knowledge That Life Becomes More Meaningful

Dr. Bill Neaves talks about both aspects of mentoring with appreciation. He spoke with pleasure about the man who replaced him as medical school dean calling occasionally to consult with him about situations at the school. Dr. Neaves enjoys this role of consultant/mentor and remembers fondly the senior colleagues who gave him their support and advice. He anticipates staying involved with the young scientists at his institute after he leaves his active role as CEO.

An inspiring example of someone who is passing on his values to others is Jim Stowers. In 1999, Jim and his wife, Virginia, had the vision of giving back to the community something more valuable than money. The Stowers Institute for Medical Research was created to produce the kind of research that will help all of mankind. It is guided by the same values and principles on which Jim Stowers built his mutual fund business: choose the best people, with the right motivation, and give them a good environment to work in. **Inspire them and let them run.**

Inspire them and let them run.

To continue with our relay race metaphor, Jim holds the baton. He chose a team that would honor his values. He carefully nurtures it until it is up to speed, ready to receive the baton and continue the race successfully. Jim Stowers did not just endow the Institute, he gave away **the gifts of his passion for being the best**.

In the final stage of our life's relay race, we bring to bear the strength and resources we have accumulated over a lifetime. When all that we have learned is shared and carried forward by those whose lives we have touched, our life acquires new meaning.

Then we are able to compound our achievements beyond ourselves.

Socrates's Plea for Authenticity

Beloved Pan, and all you other gods
Abiding hereabouts,
Grant that I may become handsome within!
May I appear to be that which I am.
May I regard wisdom as the only wealth,
And may my own wealth
Be no more than I can bear.

TIME FOR REFLECTION

Think of your life and the ways you have benefited from those who reached out and shared their lives, skills, and knowledge with you. Then think about how you have reached out. Contemplate how you would like to continue to share your experience with others.

Pepiniere

How have your grandparents or surrogate grandparents enriched your life?

As a grandparent, how do you help a child grow?

Remember the adults and older children in your neighborhood who were helpful.

Name a teacher who inspired you. What made that teacher special?

Volunteering

Remember the times in your life when you benefited from the help of a volunteer.

What skill or talent could you share with others?

Mentoring

In what way is mentoring a part of your life?

Could you benefit from a reverse mentoring situation?

The Healing Power of Doing Good

Research has shown that we need a minimum of one hour a week of "face to face" time helping someone unrelated to us. This requirement for our health and well-being is more than the random acts of kindness some of us engage in. Interconnecting with people on the internet does not count.

Spirituality and Health

A Gift to Yourself

Have you ever felt that your gift of service or time was a gift to yourself?

A Bridge Between Generations

What knowledge would you like to share to help those younger understand current events?

Passing the Baton

Have you passed the baton of your knowledge to anyone else?

How could you prepare to do this in the future?

The men who have changed the universe have
never accomplished it by changing officials,
but always by inspiring the people.

Napoleon Bonaparte

Dear Reader:

Life's relay race has many laps; long and short, swiftly run or taken at a jog or a walk. We do not know how many laps we have left. Yet, if we limit ourselves, our race may end too soon.

Albert Camus, the French writer, wrote, "In the depth of winter, I finally learned that within me there lay an invincible summer."

Are we at our limit or can we reach into ourselves for new energy and inspiration which can make us aware of our invincible summer?

It is important to pause during our race to evaluate where we are. "Aggiornamento" is an Italian word which means to update, or revitalize. When we take time out, we can pace ourselves, revitalize our lives, and find more meaning in life. We can become aware of the beauty of every day, reflected in our feelings which are mirrored back by the people around us.

We hope our book has opened up a vision into the reality of your life that will help you stretch your limits and find more meaning in life.

May you live your life with light, love, laughter, and learning.

Jack Jonathan and Sheelagh Manheim

We interviewed people to find out how our concepts and ideas applied to the diversity of experiences and changes in their lives. We are grateful for their insights which added value to our book.

Bob and Karen Brush

Married 33 years, Bob and Karen have learned to respect each others' spaces and still enjoy being together. They are parents of three adult sons who are mostly, but not totally, on their own. The Brushes are still employed; Karen as a caregiver (nurse, mother, grandmother) and Bob as a money maker (business man, father, grandfather). They are wondering how life will be once their careers wind down.

Mike Dearing

Mike Dearing says he got most of his guidance from the military and older people who were survivors of tough times like the two World Wars and the Depression. Whether it was the wisdom of his mother, a pygmy chief in the South Sea Islands, or a chief executive in a big company, Mike learned not only from words, but through the actions of the people he admired. Mike Dearing's job is to make the Stowers Institute for Medical Research a safe place for people to work in and visit. However, what really defines him is his humanity, which he expresses when he says, *"My passion is to stick up for the little man."*

Vicki Franklin

Vicki Franklin was raised in a large family with parents who had a passion for education. Although her first career dream was to be a psychologist in her physician father's psychiatric practice, she became an accountant and served as an auditor and financial analyst in corporate settings. Currently, she is an academic coach, tutor, and advocate dedicated to passing on her parents' legacy of educating young people. Her mission is: "to live, to grow, to share what I know with those who cross my path."

Stanley R. Friesen, MD, PhD

Dr. Friesen received his MD degree from the University of Kansas and his PhD in surgery from the University of Minnesota. Although he has been described as the "compleat" physician, he is a humanist with a wide range of interests and talents: pianist, artist, genealogist, world traveler, and medical mission worker. Stan Friesen has a passion for knowledge and delights in studying various fields of arts and science and finding ways to relate them. He is still active at the University of Kansas Medical School, where he shares his passion for life with the first and second year students in an effort to broaden their horizons beyond the technology of medicine.

C.W. Gusewelle

Charles Gusewelle has written for *The Kansas City Star* since 1955. His short stories and essays have appeared in *Harper's*, *American Heritage, Transatlantic Review*, and other magazines and journals. In 1977, he received the Aga Khan Prize for Fiction from the *Paris Review Foundation*. In addition, Charles has written and narrated several documentaries, one of which chronicled his remarkable trip from the source to the mouth of the Lena River in Russia. If he lived in a perfect world, Mr. Gusewelle would divide his time between Paris, a city he and his family have loved for many years, and his beloved cabin in the Ozarks.

William Barlow Neaves, PhD

Dr. Neaves is President, Chief Executive Officer and member of the Board of Directors of the Stowers Institute for Medical Research. In addition to his work at the Stowers Institute, he currently serves as a professor at the School of Medicine of the University of Missouri-Kansas City, and is a member of numerous science and medical boards of directors in the Kansas City area. Prior to joining the Stowers Institute in June 2000, Dr. Neaves served in various positions at the University of Texas Southwestern Medical Center at Dallas. He has had a distinguished career in biological science and was elected a Fellow of the American Association for the Advancement of Science in 1991.

Maggie Neff

Maggie Neff is a passionate, compassionate woman who never saw a challenge she could not overcome. With no experience in making candy, she nevertheless bought a candy store and became successful enough to put her husband through law school. When she and her husband lived in Washington D.C., she was involved in President Kennedy's inauguration and the successful election campaign of President Johnson. After she and her husband retired to Missouri, Maggie went back to college and graduated cum laude with her BA degree. She was active for many years as a board member of the Friends of Jung of Kansas City. Her ability to help the organization be successful in hosting speakers like Jean Shinoda Bolen are legendary among members of the Friends of Jung. Clearly, anyone who has Maggie on her team is a winner.

Rosemary Smithson

Rosemary Smithson's first career was writing humorous lines for Hallmark Cards, the kind of job common for young women in the 50s who were not yet married. Traditionally raised in the 40s and 50s, Rosemary became a feminist in the 60s and has worked for women's rights and equality ever since. She was one of the founders of the Women's Political Caucus, a co-founder of the Women's Political Endowment Fund, and co-founder of the Missouri Women's Leadership Coalition. Rosemary is a dedicated and serious worker for these causes, but attributes some of her success to her sense of adventure and fun. She quoted a line from a movie that seemed appropriate to the spirit of her work, *"We are making this up as we go along."* Many women who have successfully run for political office can be thankful for Rosemary's spirit of adventure.

Glenda Spellerberg

Glenda is grateful to have grown up in a rural Texas community. She feels the values of her home town and her family are the basis for her happy life. Glenda was a young mother and is a young grandmother. She feels lucky to be in a very happy marriage with a man who sees life the same way she does. They value hard work and setting an example for others. They are proud that they have been able to put two of their children through college. Glenda worked for American Century for 20 years. Following the company philosophy of "pay yourself first®" enabled Glenda to retire early and volunteer her time at VISTA, where she is working to help kids learn problem solving, team building, and self-esteem.

Giacomo Spero

Giacomo Spero is an energetic 72-year-old world traveler. He is a philosopher with a wide range of interests and experience in photography, writing, and publishing. A storyteller with a great sense of humor, he delights in the company of friends of all ages, especially when he is gathered around a big table ladened with excellent food. Mr. Spero has five children and five grandchildren who help him remain young in heart and mind.

Tina Sprinkle

Tina Sprinkle is the mother of three sons, Jesse, Cary, and Sean. She has worked in the fitness industry for over 25 years as an educator, instructor, personal trainer, business owner, and club director. She believes the body is our home on earth and, as such, is due our ultimate respect. Exercise as a ritual becomes a spiritual practice, acting as a conduit between our spiritual and physical selves. She believes when there is harmony between the mind and body, the spirit has a chance to soar.

Rose Stolowy

Rose Stolowy was born in Poland in 1912. She camc to the U.S. with her parents in 1922. She moved to Kansas City and married Sol Stolowy. They raised a family and engaged in a number of businesses. Rose started her own fabric business when her children were in school. In l982, she joined her husband in S & R Tailors, where she was the accountant for 10 years. For many years she volunteered at a local hospital. Her husband passed away in 1998. Rose still lives in her family home in Leawood, Kansas, where she engages in many hobbies and keeps in touch with her grandchildren and great-grandchildren via e-mail.

James E. Stowers

James E. Stowers is founder and chairman of the board of American Century Companies, which he started in 1958. In 1991 he wrote, with Jack Jonathan, *Yes, You Can…Achieve Financial Independence,* the 4th edition of which was published in 2004. Jim and his wife, Virginia, live in Kansas City, Missouri where they created and funded the Stowers Institute for Medical Research. The Institute, which they regard as one of the most important undertakings of their lives, aspires to be one of the world's premier biomedical research facilities with the goal of freeing humanity from gene-based diseases, such as cancer.

Peggy Wrightsman

Mother of four, wife of one, and professional writer/editor, Peggy Wrightsman believes in disproving those who dare to tell her she "can't have it all!" A former inner-city high school teacher and newspaper feature writer, Peggy has earned three undergraduate and three advanced college degrees and has studied three foreign languages. She is currently the Senior Editorial Director in Licensing at Hallmark Cards, Inc. Hcr passion for life is second only to her love of laughter. She has a deep appreciation for family, friendships, and elastic.

John Wurst

John Wurst is chairman of Henry Wurst, Inc., the family-owned Kansas City printing company now in its third generation of Wurst family management. He and his wife, Peg, raised four youngsters and are now enjoying six grandchildren. John knows the community's future is dependent on educated kids and encourages everyone who is able, to consider being a mentor. It's a good investment.

BIBLIOGRAPHY

Books

Allende, Isabel. *Aphrodite: A Memoir of the Senses.* New York: Harper Perennial, 1998.

Baker, Dan and Stauth, Cameron. *What Happy People Know.* Rodale, Inc., 2002.

Cathcart, Jim. *The Acorn Principle.* New York: St. Martin's Griffin, 1997.

Damasio, Antonio. *Looking for Spinoza.* New York: Harcourt Inc., 2003.

Davis, Laura. *I Thought We'd Never Speak Again: The Road from Estrangement to Reconciliation.* New York: HarperCollins, 2002.

Davis, Phyllis K. *The Power of Touch.* Carlsbad CA: Hay House, Inc., 1999.

Gleick, James. *Chaos: Making a New Science.* New York: Viking Penguin, Inc., 1987.

Goleman, Daniel. *Emotional Intelligence.* New York: Bantam Books, 1995.

Hoffer, Eric. *The Ordeal of Change.* New York: Harper Colophon Books, Harper and Row, 1964.

Jonathan, Jack. *Yes, You Can! Raise Financially Aware Kids.* Kansas City: Stowers Innovations, Inc., 2002.

Kassinove, H. and Tafrate, R.C. *Anger Management: The Complete Treatment Guidebook for Practitioners.* Atascaderoz CA: Impact, 2002.

Kupperman, J. *Character.* Oxford: Oxford University Press, 1991.

Merriam-Webster's Deluxe Dictionary. 10th Collegiate Edition. New York: Reader's Digest, 1998.

Norem, Julie. *The Positive Power of Negative Thinking.* New York: Basic Books, 2002.

Oldenburg, Ray. *The Great Good Place.* New York: Marlowe and Co.,1999.

Ornstein, Robert and Sobel, David. *Healthy Pleasures.* Reading MA: Perseus Books, 1989.

Owens, David. *Copies in Seconds.* New York: Simon and Schuster, 2004.

Parks, Gordon. *Choice of Weapons.* Minnesota Historical Society Press, 1986.

Pollan, Stephen. *Second Acts.* New York: Harper Resource, 2002.

Reeves, Christopher. *Nothing is Impossible: Reflections on a New Life.* New York: Random House, 2002.

Ryan, M.J. *The Power of Patience: How to Slow the Rush and Enjoy More Happiness, Success, and Peace of Mind Every Day.* Conari Press, 2002.

Seligman, Martin E.P. *Authentic Happiness.* New York: The Free Press, 2002.

Stanley, Thomas J. and Danko, William D. *The Millionaire Next Door.* New York: Pocket Books, 1996.

Stowers, James E. *Yes, You Can ... Achieve Financial Independence.* Kansas City: Stowers Innovations, Inc., 2000.

Thayer, Robert. *Calm Energy.* New York: Oxford University Press, 2001

Warner, Ralph. *Get a Life.* Berkley CA: NOLO, 2002.

White B. Rolf. T*he Great Business Quotations.* New York: Dell Publishing Company, 1986.

SPECIAL THANKS to Mary Grant, who let us publish her two poems, *"Making It Through the Night"* and *"My Home By The Sea,"* before they appeared in her soon-to-be published collection of poems.

Journals and Magazines

AARP

American Demographics

Arthritis Today

BottomLine /Personal

BottomLine/Tomorrow

Discover

The Economist

Fortune

The Futurist

Harvard Business Review

Healthtrack Wellness Program

Ions Noetic Sciences Review

Modern Maturity

Monitor on Psychology

Research News & Opportunities in Science and Theology

Science and Spirit

Scientific American Special, June 2004

Spirituality and Health

Trend Letter

Tufts University Health and Nutrition Letter

University of California, Berkeley, Wellness Letter

The Kansas City Star

The New York Times

The Wall Street Journal

Here are a few of the many, many web sites that may be of interest when you delve more deeply into the topics we discuss in our book.

The Stress Confidential Helpline: www.stresshelp.tripod.com

Love Thy Neighbor: www.unlimitedloveinstitute.org

Laughter Clubs: www.laughteryoga.org

Signature Strengths Survey: www.authentichappiness.org

The Mind and Life Institute: studying how the mind and body work together for our health: www.investigatingthemind.org

Harvard University Health Letters: www.health.harvard.edu

Tufts University Newsletter on Diet and Nutrition: www.healthletter.tufts.edu

University of California Health Letter: more information about alternative medicine: www.wellnessletter.com

Health Letter Focusing on Growing Older (from Mt. Sinai School of Medicine): www.focusonhealthyaging.com.

The Partnership for a Walkable America: www.walkableamerica.org

Want to live to be 100?: www.agingresearch.org, or www.livingto100.com

Government Information on Health: www.fda.gov

Programs to Sharpen your Mind: www.aging.usla.edu

Mutual Funds: www.americancenturyfunds.com

Stowers Innovations: for information on this book, *Yes, You Can... Achieve Financial Independence*, (4th edition), the *Stowers Financial Analysis* CD-Rom, and other publications in the Yes, You Can series: www.stowers-innovations.com

Money matters web site with investment topics: www.investorguide.com/university.html

Credit Counseling: www.nfcc.org

Information on Retirement for those 50 plus: www.aarp.org or www.bottomlinesecrets.com

Finding a Mentor: www.mentors.ca/findamentor.html

People to People International: www.ptpi.org

Travel as Education: www.elderhostel.org

Vacation as a Volunteer Activity: www.charityguide.org or www.passportintime.com

INSPIRATIONAL THOUGHTS

We have gathered from our text some of the thoughts we particularly liked. You may want to cut out the epigrams that mean the most to you and use them to help you pause during the day for reflection. Add your favorite thoughts in the blanks at the end.

The Best is Yet to Be.®

JAMES E. STOWERS

It is never too late to plant redwood trees.

SHEELAGH MANHEIM

The circle of life is like a running track on which we run our one and only race.

JACK JONATHAN

Life is light, love, laughter and learning.

JACK JONATHAN AND SHEELAGH MANHEIM

Salud, pesetas, y amor, y tiempo para gozarlos.
(Health, wealth, love, and time to enjoy them)

SPANISH PROVERB

The goal of life is not just survival,
but well-being.

ANTONIO DAMASIO

Only as you know yourself
can your brain serve you as a sharp
and efficient tool.

BERNARD BARUCH

Most folks are about as happy as
they make up their minds to be.

ABRAHAM LINCOLN

We do not stop laughing
because we grow old,
we grow old when we stop laughing.

GIACOMO SPERO

In the depth of winter,
I found there lay within me
an invincible summer.

ALBERT CAMUS

May your troubles be
Tracks in the snow,
Melting in the springtime sun.

DAVID S. VISCOTT, M.D.

Life is not measured by the number of breaths we take, but by the moments that take our breath away.

GEORGE CARLIN

God gave us memory so that we might have roses in December.

ANON

It is your relationship to life itself that brings you life.

ROBERT ORNSTEIN AND DAVID SOBEL

Wish not so much to live long as to live well.

BENJAMIN FRANKLIN

The best way to preserve your wealth is to secure your health.

DOUG LOCKWOOD

To lengthen thy life, lessen thy meals.

BENJAMIN FRANKLIN

I*f you know how to spend less than you get, you have the philosopher's stone.*

BENJAMIN FRANKLIN

W*e all of us use money, but few of us understand its true nature.*

JAMES E. STOWERS

T*ime is money, but money is not nearly as valuable without time.*

JAMES E. STOWERS

F*inancial independence is not an end, but a means to build a meaningful life.*

JAMES E. STOWERS

D*ame Fortune favors those who dare.*

OLD ITALIAN SAYING

I am so glad you are here...
It helps me realize how beautiful
my world is.

RAINER MARIA RILKE

Wishing to be friends is quick work,
but friendship is a slow ripening fruit.

ARISTOTLE

To be able to find joy in another's joy,
that is the secret of happiness.

GEORGE BERNANOS

It is one of the most beautiful compensations
of life that no man can sincerely try to
help another without helping himself.

RALPH WALDO EMERSON

He has achieved success who has lived well...
who always looked for the best in others
and given them the best he had.

BESSIE ANDERSON STANLEY

The center of human nature is rooted
in ten thousand ordinary acts of kindness
that define our days.

STEPHEN JAY GOULD

A *man's mind may be likened to a garden,*
which may be intelligently cultivated,
or allowed to run wild.

GIACOMO SPERO

I*f you have knowledge,*
let others light their candles at it.

MARGARET FULLER

T*he primary purpose of a liberal education*
is to make one's mind a pleasant place
in which to spend one's leisure.

SIDNEY J. HARRIS

T*o share our ideas with other people*
gives them legs.

GIACOMO SPERO

Discover the Good Life ™

With the *Yes, You Can* Series from Stowers Innovations

Yes, You Can... Afford to Raise a Family

Whether you're a rookie parent-to-be or a veteran with a house full of kids, the information in *Yes, You Can... Afford to Raise a Family* will show you how you can experience the priceless joy of having kids without going broke. Even if your nest is empty, you will discover new ways to think about money, look at life, and share your experiences with your grown kids.

Yes, You Can... Raise Financially Aware Kids

This one-of-a-kind book offers a new approach to helping parents teach their children the financial facts of life. Through the use of more than 100 humorous illustrations, stories, and hands-on activities *Yes, You Can... Raise Financially Aware Kids* provides enjoyable step-by-step instructions to teaching kids to appreciate the value of a dollar. Age appropriate activities fit a child's level of development, from preschool through high school.

Yes, You Can... Achieve Financial Independence

Written by James E. Stowers, one of the country's top money mangers, *Yes, You Can... Achieve Financial Independence* offers real-world strategies showing you ways to improve your financial position. Humorous illustrations and in-depth charts help to highlight many of the valuable insights.

Yes, You Can... Find More Meaning in Your Life

We are so busy earning a living, raising our family, and just getting through life, sometimes we don't pay attention to why we are doing what we are doing. *Yes, You Can... Find More Meaning in Your Life* will inspire those of all ages who wonder in quiet moments, "What is life all about?" and "Is this all there is?"